About This Book

Why is this topic important?

Trainers know that certain topics are just harder to teach than others. It's often much easier to prove compliance or mastery with programs that involve so-called "hard-skills training" (computers, software, machinery, or safety equipment). It gets tougher to demonstrate the return on the training investment with compliance-related, behavioral-based, or so-called "soft-skills training." This author recognizes that some participants come to training sessions with their own built-in fears or discomfort about the potential subject matter. *Tough Training Topics* offers trainers a way to present difficult, stressful, or even controversial material, using new plans, new tools, and techniques tested under fire on the training platform.

What can you achieve with this book?

Tough Training Topics can serve as either your off-the-shelf reference guide to help you plan for a pending training program, or it can serve as your briefcase companion just before the session begins. It can provide specific information about the topic you have to teach, when you need it, to give you the confidence to perform well under pressure.

How is this book organized?

The book contains eleven chapters and includes an Introduction and an Appendix. The first three chapters give you an overview as to what makes some topics so hard to train, how to prepare yourself to work in challenging training environments, and how to manage tough crowds in a way that works for you and for them. The central chapters provide an in-depth exploration of tough topics such as employee orientation, sexual harassment, workplace violence prevention, and substance abuse awareness. The remaining chapters cover supervisory training subjects, conflict resolution, and stress management. The final chapter offers a message of support and hope for you to thrive and succeed in your next training experience.

About Pfeiffer

Pfeiffer serves the professional development and hands-on resource needs of training and human resource practitioners and gives them products to do their jobs better. We deliver proven ideas and solutions from experts in HR development and HR management, and we offer effective and customizable tools to improve workplace performance. From novice to seasoned professional, Pfeiffer is the source you can trust to make yourself and your organization more successful.

Essential Knowledge   Pfeiffer produces insightful, practical, and comprehensive materials on topics that matter the most to training and HR professionals. Our Essential Knowledge resources translate the expertise of seasoned professionals into practical, how-to guidance on critical workplace issues and problems. These resources are supported by case studies, worksheets, and job aids and are frequently supplemented with CD-ROMs, Web sites, and other means of making the content easier to read, understand, and use.

Essential Tools   Pfeiffer's Essential Tools resources save time and expense by offering proven, ready-to-use materials—including exercises, activities, games, instruments, and assessments—for use during a training or team-learning event. These resources are frequently offered in looseleaf or CD-ROM format to facilitate copying and customization of the material.

Pfeiffer also recognizes the remarkable power of new technologies in expanding the reach and effectiveness of training. While e-hype has often created whizbang solutions in search of a problem, we are dedicated to bringing convenience and enhancements to proven training solutions. All our e-tools comply with rigorous functionality standards. The most appropriate technology wrapped around essential content yields the perfect solution for today's on-the-go trainers and human resource professionals.

Essential resources for training and HR professionals

Tough
Training
Topics

Tough Training Topics

A Presenter's Survival Guide

DR. STEVE ALBRECHT

Pfeiffer
A Wiley Imprint
www.pfeiffer.com

Published by Pfeiffer
An Imprint of Wiley
989 Market Street, San Francisco, CA 94103-1741
www.pfeiffer.com

Library of Congress Cataloging-in-Publication Data
Albrecht, Steve
  Tough training topics: a presenter's survival guide / Steve Albrecht.
     p. cm.
Includes bibliographical references and index.
   ISBN-13: 978-0-7879-7796-2 (alk. paper)
   ISBN-10: 0-7879-7796-9 (alk. paper)
   1. Business presentations. 2. Employees—Training of. 3. Training. 4. Public speaking. I. Title.
   HF5718.22.A42 2006
   658.3'124—dc22   2005022609

Acquiring Editor: Martin Delahoussaye
Director of Development: Kathleen Dolan Davies
Developmental Editor: Susan Rachmeler
Production Editor: Nina Kreiden
Editor: Rebecca Taff
Manufacturing Supervisor: Becky Carreño
Editorial Assistant: Leota Higgins

Printed in the United States of America
Printing   10   9   8   7   6   5   4   3   2   1

This book is dedicated to every trainer who overcame one of the greatest human fears—public speaking—and stood up in front of a group of total strangers (or colleagues) and just rolled with it.

CONTENTS

ACKNOWLEDGMENTS

TRAINING IS ALWAYS a collaborative effort, even if you are standing alone in front of a group. Many people contribute to your success,
long before you begin, during the session, and after it's long over. Whether
you know it or not, lots of clients and colleagues are pulling for you to do
well, both for your benefit and for theirs as well.

The information, outlines, and more accurately, the collection of slides
in this book have come partly from my experience over many years and partly
from my association with many trainers and colleagues. If you're going to borrow, borrow from the best, I always say. This list includes my father, Dr. Karl
Albrecht, who was there for Book Number 1, who gave me my first chance
to teach business writing seminars, and who then let me represent his service,
negotiation, and power thinking courses across the country.

I've learned plenty from Dr. Joseph Davis, who indoctrinated me in the
fine art of graduate school teaching and the university life. Dr. Manny Tau
provided me with equipment and software, and taught me how music is a
training room staple.

I've benefited greatly from my association with the San Diego–based
Baron Center, including Dr. S. Anthony Baron, Bobbi Baron, Dr. Suzanne

Hoffman, Ms. Jeanne McGuire, and grand marketeer, Ms. Jaimee Pittman. The Barons gave me many opportunities to develop new and cutting-edge programs and train diverse groups all around the United States and Canada. My team-teaching experiences with Suzanne and Jeanne always gave me new and useful perspectives on teaching people at every level.

Clients who have become friends include Charles Williams, from the CSAC Excess Insurance Authority; Tammie Haller and Carl Sandstrom, from the California Joint Powers Insurance Authority; Cheryl Gould, from the InfoPeople California Library Training Project; Anne Ambrose and Matt Ditzhazy, from the City of Palmdale, California; and Michael Farrow, who simply goes about saving lives every day for the Boeing Company.

I've benefited from my long associations with the American Management Association, the largest training organization in the world, and the Association of Threat Assessment Professionals, a collection of smart people who train as if lives depend on it, because they often do.

If I left out your name, know that I take a piece of you and your expertise with me every time I step on the stage. I hope to pass your knowledge and mine on to the next generation of trainers.

Everything has been said before, but since nobody listens we
have to keep going back and beginning all over again.

—André Gide

NOBODY KNOWS the troubles I've seen. Well, perhaps you do, or
you've seen the same troubles. If you've ever stood in front of a group of
strangers or colleagues, waiting for that first moment when you have to open
your mouth and say something insightful about a certain topic, then you
know my world. There is a certain sense of exhilaration when training solo,
which, when mixed with a touch of performance anxiety, can be a good and
motivating event in your life. There also exists that deep, in-the-belly pain
that comes from a sinking feeling that you, the subject, and/or the group are
out of sync, and as such, it's going to be a long session.

I have been an on-the-platform, stand-up trainer since 1987 and I have
the scars to prove it. This book was not possible for me back then; I simply
didn't have enough gravitas, enough of the gray-hair factor (or enough gray
cells, for that matter), or enough experience in front of diverse groups to be

able to say anything cogent about how to teach adults in business settings. This book is a product of my experience, good and bad, teaching training topics that were not always the most popular.

One of my more favorite movies is the Matthew Broderick teen classic, *Ferris Bueller's Day Off.* If you remember the film, there's a telling scene involving the dry-on-purpose actor/writer Ben Stein, who plays a social studies teacher at the local high school. In his usual monotonal way, Ben's trying (in vain, of course) to explain the Smoot-Hawley Tariff Act to a class full of teenagers. As the camera pans around the room, we see some kids staring at him, mouths agape, others doodling, and still others rolling their eyes in bored disbelief.

My favorite student has his head down on his desk, and we see him come back awake after a nice little nap, leaving a small puddle of drool in his wake.

Whether you're new to the training environment or an old hand at it, you may have had the adult version of this lad in one of your sessions.

Let's face it: some training programs are fun to go to and others are not. Because of the intensity of the subject matter or the potential liability attached to some training topics, no amount of icebreakers, group activities, or snappy videos will make cod liver oil taste like chocolate pudding.

Lots of people want to go to the outdoor teamwork seminars involving ropes and trees, the stress management courses held at resort hotels, or the "Humor in the Workplace" sessions, featuring "Robin Williams on Management."

Few people want to go to training programs on sexual harassment; diversity problems (especially if the training is in response to some incident); issues related to safety or security compliance; or concerning employee behavior problems.

All this I know to be true from painful experience. Having been one of the pioneers in the field of workplace violence prevention training, I have stood in front of less-than-friendly groups of supervisors or employees, ready to hear how I think they're all ready to "go postal."

Critical Success Factors

The next time you're faced with dosing your groups with spoonfuls of bad-tasting training medicine, consider the following ideas before you take the platform:

- Get early management buy-in before you start any program. The participants *must* know the senior staff believes in the validity of the training. It helps to have a senior executive on hand to introduce you and the program and, better yet, to attend each session.

- Admit early on to the participants that the subject is tough because it either lacks glamour or will require some focus on potential negatives. "We may talk about some challenging issues today. I want everyone to know this is a safe learning environment and what you say here, stays here."

- Know your subjects intimately. Be ready to answer questions with a timely and legally accurate response. You don't have to suggest you know everything, but your credibility gets damaged if you're not seen as the expert in the room.

- Change their concept of the material from a "You" mindset (as in, "This will be *your* problem. . . .") to an "Us" mindset (as in, "This is an issue that affects all of *us*. . . .").

- The tougher the subject, the more you need to change the learning format. Don't just stand up there and read from the book, manual, or handouts. Do magic tricks, show videos, provide group tabletop exercises, use three-member role plays (manager-employee-observer), or try a bit of self-deprecating humor to suggest your take on the material is not always "by the book."

- Elicit case studies, solutions that have worked, or individual problems that the group might identify with themselves. Spot the employee leaders in the group and have them provide the specifics that make the solutions you've just taught seem viable.

- Don't threaten them with the "law book" (civil liability or litigation) or the "rule book" (company policies and procedures). Remind the participants of the seriousness of your subjects and the potential consequences; don't beat them over the heads with fear factors.

- End on a positive note, especially with a carefully selected humorous story, an upbeat case, or an incident that showed how training or compliance worked well.

The Scope of This Book

This book covers a lot of ground. *Tough Training Topics* spans a variety of complex training subjects, including new-employee orientation sessions, sexual harassment prevention, drug and alcohol policies, workplace violence prevention, coaching and counseling skills, performance evaluations, progressive discipline and hostile termination techniques, stress management, safety and security education, and conflict resolution.

Each of the training subject-matter chapters will use the following design model throughout:

Key. What is the essence of this subject? What makes it tough to train?

Usual Audience. Who will attend? Executives, managers, supervisors, frontline employees? Separately or together? Union members? Licensed, professional people? Blue-collar workers? A majority of non-English speakers?

Best Length. How long is too long? How short is too short?

Basic Training Themes. What subject needs to be taught?

Current Organizational Policies. What exists, in writing or in draft form, as a policy or procedure related to this topic?

The Organizational Culture and Climate. Is the culture supportive of this training topic? Is the current climate plagued with hostility, or is it nourishing and supportive?

The (Real) Purpose of the Program. What has happened? Was there an incident, event, or reason that brings you in front of this group?

Their Learning Keys. What must you cover? Company policies, definitions, reporting procedures, the manager or supervisor's responsibilities, employee do's and don'ts, and so forth.

Your Teaching Keys. What teaching approach will work best? Lecture, video, group or individual exercises, Q&A style, hands-on learning, and so forth.

Your Success Tools. Do you plan to use PowerPoint™ slides, a related video, some recent examples from the media or business world, a design based on explaining the current policy in detail, handouts, exercises, pre- and post-tests, or other methods?

Potholes and Sandpits. What topics do you need to avoid? What's the absolute wrong way to teach this material?

Some Fine Points. What are the little things you can do to make the program a success, ranging from meeting the participants before the session, to taking a tour of their facility, to reading the feedback sheets from past sessions?

Sample Leader's Guide/Training Module Outlines and Lecturettes. Some of the training topics in this book demand more depth than others. I've made certain assumptions that you will already have some familiarity with employee orientation programs and Supervisor 101/management development/supervisor improvement programs, having either taught them or attended them. To help with the more challenging topics—sexual harassment, workplace violence (my usual training area), drugs and alcohol, conflict resolution, and stress management—I've provided either Leader's Guide materials, FAQs (Frequently Asked Questions), or "lecturettes."

The Leader's Guides are broken down into modules, so you can either glean more information, pull some facts and figures, or simply re-educate yourself on the topic. The FAQs go a bit deeper into the subject and may help you when it comes to fielding tough questions from the crowd. And the lecturettes are short articles about the topics that you can use to design your slides, fill in any knowledge gaps, or pull specific material from.

Sample Slides. I've provided some core slides, which I've labeled, somewhat grandiosely, as the Essential Eight, the Necessary Nine, the Essential Eleven, and so on. Think of them as the "sourdough starter" for your own bread-baking process. These slides have more than enough content to get you started. In fact, I've violated most of the Articles of the Faithful when it comes to slide design. *There is way too much text on some of the slides; this is intentional.* You should feel free to break up the content of the slides in a flow and format that works best for you. Longer programs might need more slides; shorter ones may not require handouts.

You can add to the slides or subtract from them, depending on your needs, the needs of the client, and the way you want to connect with the audience. With a bit of research on the various cutting-edge issues for each of these topics, you can fill out your own slide programs nicely, simply by starting with my cores.

Readers

This book will appeal to anyone who must present difficult material to less-than-thrilled audiences.

This teaching and training group certainly includes in-house trainers, especially those who make up a "Training Department of One" and must teach nearly every program themselves. Other readers include internal consultants, who often must justify their existence by staying on the cutting edge with their presentations and topics. Of course, the book will appeal to outside trainers and external consultants, especially the well-traveled, bi-coastal veterans who, when asked by their clients, say, "*Of course* I can teach that subject for you!"

It may help the freelancers, those sole proprietor trainers and consultants, who make their livings locally, as "freeway fliers," driving between training or teaching assignments for various government, college, or private-sector clients.

Last, the book can help individual managers and supervisors, or even budding supervisors from the HR staff, who may be tasked to (read that as forced into) teach specific programs on certain subjects, and who don't have a clue as to what to say or how to say it.

This book is for a certain niche of internal or external consultant/trainers, college faculty members (who freelance or have a training or consulting practice on the side), or an HR-oriented employee, supervisor, or manager. It will also appeal to attorneys, who serve as either in-house advisors or outside counsel, and who must teach these hard subjects on a regular basis.

This book does not offer much sales or marketing advice as to how to convince your internal or external clients to hire you or bring you in to teach training. Let's face it, tough training topics, as must-do, must-have subjects for many organizations, have always been driven by two concerns: the cost/benefit analysis and as a response to *events*.

We usually conduct sexual harassment training in response to a rise in the number of incidents reported to HR. We usually teach drug and alcohol awareness training for supervisors after arrests, accidents, or a steep rise in theft cases. We present programs on safety procedures, security awareness, or workplace violence prevention programs, not because we want to, but because we have to, based on these issues rearing their often-ugly heads.

Our Marching Plan

In writing this book, I've made certain assumptions about your training programs and the locations where you will present them. I make these assumptions here and now, so I don't have to re-clarify myself each time I discuss a certain tough training topic. In general, for each program:

1. You will be using a laptop computer and projector, equipped with Microsoft PowerPoint™. While overhead transparencies are still in use, most participants dislike the format (the white light glares on the screen during the transitions, the lack of color, the older fonts, the ever-crooked alignment, the heat and hum of the projectors, the bulb burnouts, and so on). If you still use transparencies for your programs, there's a good chance this will be reflected negatively in your feedback sheets.

2. If you need it, you will be able to get access to a VHS VCR/TV to play any videotapes connected to your program.

3. You will have access to easel pads, masking tape, and marking pens.

4. Participants will be indoors, in some formal or informal training room environment, that is, conference room, classroom, hotel meeting room, auditorium, community center, employee learning center, or other indoor place. Since I don't do training programs outside (ropes courses, confidence courses, outdoor team-building

exercises), I'll stick to what I know about controlling the inside environment.

5. Let's agree on the flexibility of our language. No matter what I call them in the book: the attendees, the participants, the audience, the folks, the group, the crowd, or the members, they are all the same—people you will train, using some program and format, and covering a time span from 30 minutes to one week in length. Further, I will use these terms interchangeably to describe a training experience of some duration: course, class, session, seminar, meeting, presentation, program, or workshop. I will also use these terms to describe us: trainer, presenter, seminar leader, course leader, program leader, facilitator, or speaker.

6. You will usually provide some form of training handouts to the participants: copies of your PowerPoint™ slides stapled, spiral- or comb-bound pages, or in a three-ring notebook; copies of policies and procedures, new-employee manual pages, instruction sheets, one-page cheat sheets, laminated cards, and so forth. The format depends on what you need or want them to walk away with after you're done. I'm fully aware that it's not uncommon to see all of your hard efforts on the handouts deposited in the trash can as people exit the room. This helps to support the idea that some training topics are just tough and some people don't want or need a reminder of what they just sat through. We use handouts for those who do want to review the materials again and to create a permanent record in HR of what was taught.

7. As trainers, we often serve at the feet of the master—the dreaded Feedback Sheet. Like it or not, many clients use feedback sheets as a barometer for training success. For many of them (subconsciously, I believe), it's more important that the group enjoyed the process or gave positive feedback about the trainer than if the group actually learned any demonstrable behavioral changes. As such, I will refer to the need to train well, to get high marks on feedback sheets, to get future work. There are certain techniques for doing this and

while "manipulating the crowd" sounds terrible, it's your duty to make sure they have the chance to highlight your hard work for others. See Chapter Eleven for more on feedback sheets.

8. You will be working for a "client" in one derivation or another, either as an external trainer, consultant, HR generalist, or attorney, providing your training services to their group. Or you are employed as an internal trainer, providing your expertise inside your own organization to fellow employees.

It's with these assumptions in mind that we spring forth and decipher what makes some training topics so tough to teach and, more importantly, what we can do to make it more possible for everyone, either as trainers or participants, to enjoy the experience.

What Makes Some Training Topics So Tough?

I am so clever that sometimes I don't understand
a single word of what I am saying.

—Oscar Wilde

Key

This chapter introduces the trainer to two obvious ideas: (1) certain topics are not popular with training course participants and (2) so what do you do about it? The reasons behind the first point are often based on the past experiences or the current work culture of the participants. And the second point asks, "What are you willing to do, as the presenter of the moment, to make their session positive, dynamic, and even memorable?"

You're the training director, manager, or head of a one-person training department. The assignment today is to conduct new employee orientation (again) to those bright and shining faces sitting before you, pens at the ready, eager to learn. They're a willing training audience because they have to be one. They laugh at your jokes, nod alertly at your most cogent points, take copious notes, review the material you hand out to them, and promise to abide by the phone book–thick set of policies and procedures in their new kit bag. You leave the training platform feeling like the world is your PowerPoint™.

You're an outside training consultant, in-house company attorney, or the corporate counsel. You find yourself standing in a room full of department heads, managers, and frontline supervisors. They've gathered here for the sole purpose of sitting through the yearly sexual harassment lecture. Perhaps the culture of the organization has shifted a bit, boundaries are being blurred, and the media-driven times have given some employees the "freedom" to speak their minds.

It's time to tighten up on this behavior. It's time, says senior management, to round up the usual suspects and hit them over the head with the law book again. So you start your lecture on the do's and don'ts of quid pro quo versus the sexually harassing or hostile work environment. By the end, you've successfully divided the room into equal thirds: one group that feels embarrassed for being male, one group that feels embarrassed for being female, and one group that doesn't know why they're suddenly angry for having given you two hours of their time.

Perhaps you're an outside consultant and an HR generalist and you've been asked to conduct a sexual harassment prevention course for frontline employees. You study up on the latest litigation sagas and get the dollar figures right in your mind. After about your third story involving some hapless firm that was sued successfully for an egregious violation, you realize your approach has made the lights go on for several of the more entrepreneurial participants. After the course, several of them take long lunches and head to their favorite labor law attorneys, convinced they now have million-dollar cases.

These are only a few of the potential training room disasters that await presenters who work for or with organizations. This book offers a lifeline for these scenarios and others for which the topics and the audiences are tough.

The definition of a "tough training topic" is this: It's often driven by a negative event in the organization. It often features a subject that is seen or has been historically perceived by the stakeholders (the attendees, the client who brings the trainer in, and even the trainer) as difficult to teach, hard to sit through, and laden with emotional or legal baggage. Attendance is often mandatory. The group's reaction to both the subject and the trainer's delivery can range from polite indifference to outright hostility.

People come to tough training topics with preconceptions, misconceptions, and apprehensions. The featured subject may remind them of their vulnerability in the workplace, including their lack of knowledge about the issue, fear of discipline or termination for violations, or the fear of either being victimized by others or even falsely accused, in the case of significant behavioral concerns.

Attending training for behavioral subjects can dredge up unpleasant memories from, with, or by past perpetrators. I have taught client-mandatory sexual harassment programs with both past victims and documented harassers in the same room. I have presented drug and alcohol programs with people in the room who had just finished rehabilitation stints for substance abuse. I taught a workplace violence program to an organization that had just suffered through an employee's suicide. The wife of the victim (a man who had threatened her and other employees) was ordered to go by her employer, against my express wishes. I never mentioned the case to the group, although they all knew about it and kept looking at her for her reaction throughout the class. When she came to me sobbing after the first break, I told her she could leave and I would square it with her supervisor. She thanked me and left and I finished another tough training topic in a tough environment.

Adult Learning Methods: Revising Kirkpatrick

In 1959, University of Wisconsin professor Don Kirkpatrick put it best when he described the impact of training on the classroom participants as reaching one of four possible levels (Alliger & Janak, 1989):

1. Reaction—measures how those who participate in the program react to it.

2. Learning—the extent to which participants change attitudes, improve knowledge, and increase skill as a result of attending the program.

3. Behavior—the extent to which a change in behavior has occurred because the participants attended the training program.

4. Results—the final results that occurred because the participants attended the program.

Well, with kudos and respect to Mr. K, here's "Dr. Steve Albrecht's Take on the Kirkpatrick Model," in the light of 21st century thinking.

Level 1: They Came. They Sat Through Your Lecture. They Left.

Maybe they liked the trainer, the fact they got out of work for some span of time, or just the doughnuts and coffee. Maybe they hated the subject or the content of the program, yet enjoyed the trainer's approach. Maybe the reverse was true and a ham-fisted course leader ruined an otherwise good program. Perhaps the course content or the presenter failed to inspire them to change, adjust, or improve their behavior or skills.

Level 2: They Came. They Sat Through Your Lecture. They Learned Enough to Pass the Post-Test or Demonstrate Some Basic Level of Competence or Understanding in the Near Future.

Here, the goal is simply compliance and the course leader helped them reach it. The order of the day was "Stop doing X, Y, or Z" or "Start doing A, B, and C." By various means (sheer personality, a solid design, interesting exercises), the instructor got this group to learn one or more points and demonstrate this new knowledge. Whether they can "keep on keeping on" or whether they revert back to their old ways remains to be seen. The hope is, of course, that these new tools, skills, behaviors, policies, or rules will stick beyond the glow of the moment in the training environment.

Level 3: They Came. They Sat Through Your Lecture. They Learned Enough to Want to or Be Able to Change, Improve, or Modify Their Own Behavior as a Manager or Employee, Almost Immediately.

At this level, the training program resonated with the participants enough for them to see the wisdom of the materials and presentation. Collectively, many of them begin to apply the knowledge, tools, or policies in visible or measurable ways. For example, safety problems or accidents diminish, individual production or performance improves across the board, and new policies or procedures bear fruit in terms of the employees' or managers' individual behaviors.

Level 4: They Came. They Sat Through Your Lecture. And They Learned Enough to Want to or Be Able to Change the Way Their Department or Organization Does Its Business, Starting Today.

Here, the group leaves satisfied and begins to work synergistically to improve the overall performance of their respective work group, team, or department. Changes are both visible and invisible, but the performance improvement is undeniable either way. We see evidence of compliance, cohesion, communication, and perhaps even the reduction of conflict between group members. Managers and frontline supervisors find it easier to remind their people of key points, outcomes, or tools from the training program and, as a result, the course and concepts develop good word-of-mouth momentum. Future sessions are well-attended and the successful training creates more success stories as it permeates the organization and its personnel.

Training at the Level One stage can best be described as the "Fizzle Factor" in action. The program simply died on the vine. At our Goal Level, which is Level Four, however, the trainer has accomplished his or her mission:

- Gathered the various stakeholders to discuss the issues;

- Created a convincing and/or entertaining method (humor, videos, stories, individual or group exercises) to educate them about the subject, policy, or procedure at hand;

- Used methods to help the participants recap what they learned (pre- and post-tests, reviews, feedback, Q&A sessions, and other methods); and

- Checked back at intervals (one week, one month, six months, or whatever) to see how the participants are actually using what they learned on the job, alone, in their work groups, with their customers, and with their bosses.

Training at Level One is probably the toughest on both parties—the trainer and the trainees. A lack of engagement on either of their parts makes for a long morning or afternoon. And here are the hardest "tough training topic" questions of all:

- How do you prove a negative?
- How do you prove what you taught them stopped their negative behavior?
- How do you know, absent of a repeat of the negative event that brought you to the front of the room in the first place, that you've succeeded?

The hard answers to each? You don't. If you put a locking device on the steering wheel of your car and you come out the next morning, and your car is still there, what have you proved? Nothing! Either the thief walked by, saw the lock, and was deterred enough to find another car to steal, or he never walked by at all.

And so it goes with tough training topics; you may never know or be able to prove that what you said or did with the group had an impact. But you keep getting up in front of them because you know that, while your results may be hard to measure, they exist, and what you do is important, now and in their future.

Content Versus Delivery

The goal of any training program for every participant should be to retain the material and be able to apply it. Training is not effective simply because the trainer, the internal/external client, or even the feedback sheets say it was. It's only effective when we see a change, even a slight one, in the participants' behaviors. They *stop* doing something they have been doing that was detrimental to their health, safety, or work performance. They *start* doing something different, in terms of improving their job productivity or performance, by using a new skill or technique you've just taught them. Or they keep on keeping on, continuing to work at a level that satisfies them and their organization, using what you have taught them as a benchmark into the future.

So when it comes to the question between where you should put your design emphasis—content (*what* you tell them) versus delivery (*how* you tell them)—the answer is: It depends. (Not only is this always a useful phrase when one of your attendees poses a head-scratching question, it's also completely true with most life issues; it *does* depend.)

One of my many flaws as a beginning trainer was over-preparation. My exercises were too complicated, my lectures were too long and complex, and my breaks too few. I was convinced that because I had a lot of information about my various subject areas, that I had to cram all of what I knew into the heads of the participants. This led to my expanding the content so much that I took all of the life (read that as fun) out of the program.

The kinder feedback sheets had the same themes: "Smart guy. Knows his subject. Lots of material. Seemed kind of rushed. Hard to know what to use in all that. Kind of like drinking from a fire hose." The less-than-kind feedback sheets were less polite: "Talks way too much. Not enough hands-on learning. Too much, too fast. Who cares anyway? I just came for the food and the overtime."

Sadly (for the people who suffered through my first years on the platform), I took these words to mean that I needed to prepare even more material and work even harder to get my point across. Finally, some kind and generous training peers took me aside and pointed at my inches-thick personal leader's guides and said, "Lighten up. It's not how smart you are, it's how smart you can make them, in the time you have."

And of course they were right. In my rush to fill the course time span with content, I took out all the fun. I soon discovered that it's all about balance—and something called the Strength-Weakness Irony, which says:

"Your strength, when taken to an extreme, becomes a weakness."

I was smart enough, but that's never enough. Too much taxation of participants' gray matter, without the insertion of something memorable, makes for a training session that is lifeless and dull. I had to learn how to *spice up* the delivery and *whittle down* the content to its most useful essence.

In the battle between Content versus Delivery, there are four distinct camps:

1. High in Content—High in Delivery

2. Low in Content—High in Delivery

3. High in Content—Low in Delivery

4. Low in Content—Low in Delivery

We can define "content" as the type of material presented, the depth to which it is covered, the complexity of the information, and whether it is data, information, policies, or procedures that are made "sticky," that is, memorable later.

We can define "delivery" as the way we present the material: using humor, stories, group or individual exercises, team-building or problem-solving events, videos, magic tricks, lectures and lecturettes, pre-reading or post-training work, pre- or post-tests, or anything short of lighting a portion of yourself on fire and sprinting around the room, to make the session memorable later.

Which of the above four is the best or worst for the participants depends on their respective points of view. From where they sit, there are advantages to some of these four, but not all. When you review the list again, the rank is probably fairly close to how most participants want it.

High in Content—High in Delivery

This is good for them and good for you, as the presenter. They come away saying, "That was not too bad, enjoyable even. I learned a lot; it wasn't too painful. The time went by quickly and there were some valuable ideas."

For you, this is the good news, in terms of the feedback. The bad news is that this area requires the hardest effort and preparation for you as a presenter. This is where the now-popular request for information and entertainment becomes "infotainment." You must have a deep and thorough knowledge of your material and you must present it in a way that stimulates, amuses, and connects with your audience. Training at this level means you give a *performance,* not just a program.

While working at this level requires the most pre-training effort for you, it also provides the biggest payoff: great feedback, high levels of retention, higher client satisfaction, and "viral marketing," meaning that people tell other people and future courses fill up through good word of mouth.

Low in Content—High in Delivery

The good news is that this training approach tends to be the most popular with almost every audience who experiences it. There's laughter, energy, good feelings, and the whole thing starts and ends on a high note.

The bad news is that they often leave without having learned a bloody thing. When asked to give feedback to those who ask how it went, they say, "It was great! We sang songs, made paper hats, and laughed at some funny jokes!" It's only when they're asked what they actually learned or remember about the program that the head scratching and the puzzled looks begin.

This is one of the hardest knocks on people who make their living doing what could be called "pure" motivational speaking. This approach is all sizzle and no steak, with a good-looking man or woman, with nice hair and straight white teeth, ranting and sweating on the stage, feverishly pumping the crowd to "go and live their dreams" or similar swell-sounding but hard-to-apply messages.

This approach is also popular with a certain strata of trainers who were taught or who believe that people need to be doing some kind of group or individual activity every five minutes or it's not really training. "You can't just talk to them. You have to *engage* them to get them to learn anything. Studies tell us this, you know."

The irony of the low content—high delivery approach is that sometimes the participants feel later as if they have been cheated. Their good times and good fun masked the fact that they didn't actually learn anything new, acquire necessary skills, or accomplish much of any importance. Those participants who see their time as valuable and want to know more about the subjects in question will demand more from the presenter than just good feelings at the end.

High in Content—Low in Delivery

This was my old disease and I had it bad. Another tag for this approach is the "Brainy College Professor Model." Here, the noted astronomer, physicist, or Nobel Laureate in romance languages working at the prestigious university enters a lecture hall filled with two hundred students, picks up a piece of chalk, turns to the chalkboard, and starts lecturing. Two or so hours later, the lecture is finished and the professor turns and leaves the building. Lots of information, zero interaction with the students, who are supposed to be enthralled by the sheer brain power in the room with them.

As a training approach, the heavy-on-the-information, straight lecture style can lead to brutal feedback sheets. It's not uncommon to see people in the audience simply throw down their pens in disgust, as the information overload has made it too difficult to take notes or keep up with the lecture.

The more complex the subject, the more this is the wrong way to teach it. Most people will start out trying to keep up, but after a few hours, where they've had little or no opportunity to engage with the presenter, ask questions, or catch their collective breaths, they will just tune it all out.

The irony of this approach is that the content experts think it's the *audience's fault* if they get bored, can't assimilate the material, or otherwise slump in their seats from intellectual exhaustion. "They're just not as smart as I am" is their rationalizing mantra. "They should learn to adjust to my lecturing style, not the other way around" is a common justification for putting people's feet to sleep.

Low in Content—Low in Delivery

This is the worst of the worst; no one learned anything and it was boring to boot. This approach is most common with novice trainers who break all the rules: stand in front of the projector and block the slides; mumble in a monotone; consult notes frequently, so they get a good view of the top of his or her head; turn away from the group and simply read the content of each and every slide verbatim; forget to give breaks; wander off the topic; fail to ask or answer questions; and close the session in a discomforting way, for example, "I hope I didn't bore you too much. Hah hah. . . ."

Sometimes, trainers trapped at this level don't mean to be this bad; they just don't know any better or can't help themselves. I once worked with a colleague who was earnest and smart and nice and a lousy trainer. This person couldn't tell a joke without blowing the punch line, couldn't come up with one relevant story to further illustrate the content of a slide, and couldn't stop standing in front of the projector, ever. After one year of trying, the person gave up and realized that some people are destined to train and others are not. It's not a reflection of any personality flaw; it's just a stylistic issue.

When you have a flair for this business it shows, and when you don't, even after numerous attempts and much coaching and support, that shows too. Audiences will be kind to rookies to a point, but when some of the less tactful participants smell blood in the water, it may be time to pack your marking pens and try something less taxing to the thickness of your skin.

The story of "Goldilocks and the Three Bears" was more right than we know: Sometimes, too short is too short and too long is too long. Sometimes, you need handouts and sometimes you don't. You can speak too fast on some issues and not fast enough on others. If you feel passionate about the point, you can go on for a good long time, in an animated way, and still keep your audience's attention throughout. Or, if you're not too committed to the ideas or the teaching method to get them across, the audience will sense this as well.

Perhaps some real perspective about all this will help. I attend a number of training seminars and learning programs each year, as part of my consulting work, to review the efforts of my own training subcontractors, and for my own personal or professional development (sharpening the saw, as Stephen Covey would put it).

After years of sitting through hours and hours of other people's training approaches, styles, and formats, I've boiled it down to this theme, which I provide to each audience I teach today:

> We will be here together for eight hours. I'm going to talk to you and with you about a number of things. I plan to share with you what I believe, and your organization believes, you will need to know about this subject. It may shock some of you to learn that not everything I say will be useful to you. I won't be offended if you don't take copious notes or hang on my every word. About half of what I tell you will probably leave your heads as soon as we're done today. That's human nature and it says something about the way we are all bombarded by too many messages, too many good ideas to remember at once. So here's all I'm asking of you today: If you can take one or two important concepts or key points from our morning session and one or two important concepts or key points from our afternoon session, then it will be a good day for both of us. I'm willing to go hard to teach the first 50 percent, so if you

promise to go hard to learn the next 50 percent, then we'll get out of here on time and it will have been a good day.

Ten Ingredients That Make for a Tough Training Day

The following set of disappointments can make your time on the training platform painfully long, no matter how much experience you have. Better to see them here now and either take steps to prevent them later, or be ready to sidestep their impact when they arise (and they will).

1. Bad Warm-Up Act

You've penned a carefully crafted bio sheet, listing just the right mix of education and accomplishments, so as to build early rapport with your audience. Your introducer flubs the pronunciation of your name, skips sections in your introduction, ad-libs it, throws in some of his or her own jokes, and rings the death bell with witty lines like, "He or she will try not to bore you too much" or "I hope nobody falls asleep, since it's right after lunch."

The cure here is to be politely but forcefully direct. Meet with your introducer several minutes before the session and say, "Here's my bio sheet. I put a lot of work into it so I can connect with these folks right away. I've put my name phonetically here at the top [a good idea if your name is even slightly hard to pronounce] and I'd like you to please read this word-for-word, just as you see it here. If you have any questions as you're reviewing it, please let me know. Thanks very much for making me look good here today."

2. Bad Room

A hard and harsh fluorescent light shines right over the screen, obliterating the majestic colors of your slides. There is a high-ceilinged echo effect in various places where you stand. Outside, the gardeners are hard at work with their leaf blowers or, if you're truly blessed, the city has chosen today to tear up the nearby street with a jackhammer. The architect conveniently asked the builder to install several formidable concrete pillars in the path between the audience and your podium. While these are great for load-bearing, they force people to crane their necks around cement to get a view of you if you move even three feet in either direction.

This problem is best answered by Teddy Roosevelt, who said: "Do the best you can, with what you have, where you are." Don't let a bad design hem you in as a moving trainer or otherwise ruin your day. Don't harp on it with the group. Make a few humorous asides about the kitchen noise or the harsh glare from the curtain-less windows and move on to your business.

When it comes to the visual design of the room, know that nothing is necessarily permanent. If you can, start by making bold changes, moving chairs into different seating arrangements other than just rows. If the screen is not fixed, move it to another part of the room, even behind you, and turn the chairs around. Aim your projector on a bare, white wall, instead of using their screen. Cover the windows with taped-together easel pad sheets. Improvise, adapt, and be creative. It's your space for that time span.

3. Bad Equipment

The microphone whistles when you get too close to the air conditioning vent, which is giving off a loud but sickly hum of warm air. Your computer has chosen this moment in its life to start giving you error messages. Your projector decides to act up, flickers, and then goes dark.

First off, know your equipment. Always make certain you have all the necessary power cords, extension cords, and power strips with you in your trainer's bag. Don't rely on the client to have the necessary power supplies nearby. In some training rooms, the power outlets are in the floor, in others they're on the wall near the screen area, and in still others, nowhere to be found.

If you have any hint of technical problems as you're setting up, be ready to preface your opening remarks with what I call "the 5 percent warning." Here, you simply remind the group, with a smile, that electronics, like life, rarely work the way you planned. If they have any familiarity with computers, they'll sympathize, since it's probably happened to them as well. If any technical glitches do arise, it may help to ask, "Is there a computer doctor in the house?" Most groups have at least one PC or audiovisual aficionado in their midst, so perhaps he or she can come to your rescue.

While this person is fiddling with the connections, march on, switching subjects or directions if you need to, until the break, when you can devote more time and energy to any repairs.

4. Bad Slides or Handouts

You were in a hurry, so you didn't notice the client's company name is mis-spelled on the title pages of two hundred copies of the handouts. Or the client has copied your masters in the wrong order, skipping some pages and switching others. You notice not one but several typos on both the slides and the handouts (since one is a derivation of the other). The colors for the slides, which looked so perfect in the light of your office, look washed out or harsh in the light of the training room.

Some things you can control and others you can't. Typos and bad slide designs are certainly under your control. Have other people look at your materials, both on the computer screen and in print, before you present them or make the necessary handout copies. Other eyes will almost always catch poor grammar, misspellings, or other typos that you miss by being too close to the material.

If the slide color scheme doesn't fit the room lighting, jump right into PowerPoint™ and make the background color changes on the fly. This is yet another reason to get to the training room early enough to set up and test the slides in that light. Simply changing the background color can do a lot to improve the look and quality of the slides.

5. Bad Participant(s)

As Chapter Three will illustrate in traumatic detail, there is no shortage of stories about how certain participants can make for a long training day. While teaching a negotiating seminar on the east coast, I had three officers from a trade union in attendance. During the three-day program, they returned from each lunch break loud and drunk. They fought with each other (the alcohol talking) and, at one point, they all got into a shoving match with other participants during a case study exercise. I asked them to leave and they did. They asked for a refund from the client and didn't get it.

My father, Karl Albrecht, tells a classic story about a frontline employee who came to one of his service management seminars. Once the program began, she made a big display of showing her displeasure at being "forced" to attend the "mandatory" training. She turned her chair in the opposite direction of the other attendees, crossed her arms, and stared at the far wall. My dad asked her if she wanted to leave and she said, "I can't because this is mandatory training. But nobody told me I had to participate." He agreed and asked if anyone else felt as upset about being there as she did. No one raised his or her hand.

Karl then said, "I'm sorry you're upset with your situation. I'm going to continue. You're welcome to join us at this table here if you want, or you're free to go back to work. I'll tell your supervisor personally that you had my permission to sit this one out." At that point, with all of her peers looking at her in disgust and amusement, she decided to join with the others. She got through the day unscathed and so did everyone else.

The point is: You can't change their personalities and you can't change their views of their world. You can only offer to provide a safe and comfortable learning environment.

6. Bad Energy

Here, it's not necessarily one or more unruly participants, it's the whole room. Perhaps you got started late, due to problems with traffic or equipment, or the room was locked when you arrived. Perhaps people continue to trickle in once you have begun and this disrupts your thoughts. Perhaps someone has said something negative at the start and the room has suddenly turned cold. Perhaps your best icebreakers, jokes, magic tricks, exercises, and room energizers have all fallen flat. It happens and it's not fun.

Sometimes it *is* your fault and sometimes it is what it is. Comedians and other live performers talk about bad energy in the crowds and how, on some nights, you just don't connect. When faced with this scene, training pros keep on keeping on, continuing to try to salvage the experience with their best materials and best efforts. Novice trainers turn sullen, rationalize that it's the fault of the crowd, and blame everyone and everything except themselves.

Sometimes it's you and sometimes it's them and sometimes it's a combination of both. If a joke falls flat, smile and move on. Deal with early hostility in a positive, professional, and diplomatic way. Don't lose your objectivity by losing your cool. Debating endlessly with a hostile participant will never win you any points with the other audience members. They will end up resenting you and the other person. This is not a nightclub, so you don't win laughs by engaging with or putting down any hecklers. Be a pro and work through to the end. There's always another day, another group.

7. Bad Corporate Climate

Hostile, argumentative, and apathetic crowds are not just the names of punk rock bands; they're reasons why you can be set up to fail. Like the Bad Energy problem, the culture of the client organization is usually toxic rather than nourishing. Poisonous organizations—where people don't communicate on purpose, don't get along with each other by choice, or where there is a high degree of labor-management tension—don't often respond to training subjects very well.

This aura of hostility can come across to you, in the comments you hear from the participants before you begin the program and in the questions you get during the breaks, "Why doesn't my boss have to attend this?" or "Are you only here because of some kind of incident or problem?"

I've had experiences where people are required to come to mandated training and they simply sign the roster and leave. I've had groups who came in and wore their sunglasses inside for the length of the training. I've taught programs to people who challenged me with increasingly hostile questions right from the start, as if I was the enemy, even though I was just an outsider with a projector.

It's challenging and nerve-wracking once the group starts saying things like, "None of this stuff you're telling us will do any good. Nothing will change around here. We've tried doing this before and it always ends up back the same way as usual."

One way to get these kinds of groups on your side is to wave the white flag early. Here's what I usually say to tough crowds, whose anger has been fueled by past events or experiences:

I hear what you're all saying to me. I know it's important to you that management gets your message too. What I propose is that we go ahead with the training as planned and I will start adding your comments to a series of "Parking Lot" easel pages. I promise to type these up and provide them to senior management. I won't try to fool you by saying that you'll see immediate changes based on your comments or requests. I will, however, be your messenger for these important issues.

8. Bad Introductory or Closing Comments by Senior Management

One of the ways you can often detect both bad climates and bad leaders is by listening to the opening or closing comments by the senior person who opens or closes the training session. This person may stay for only a few minutes at the beginning (just enough time to do significant damage to the group's morale or your overall message) or this person may show up again at the end of the program (to douse the group with ice water).

I had one session where the HR director started off a sexual harassment program for all employees by telling a truly tasteless (and potentially sexually harassing) joke. When it fell absolutely flat, she said, "And now here's Steve to teach you what not to do or say at work." When she left, I started by saying to the group, "Rule Number One: Don't do what she just did!"

It was a risk, to go after her in that manner, and it breaks one of my cardinal rules of not making sport of senior management. But, with the air suddenly thick with tension, I felt I had to do something to get them on my side and quickly. They laughed and we moved on.

In another program where I facilitated a real-time tabletop exercise for a disaster response/business continuity situation, the director of the group watched the entire exercise play out with little comment. At the end of the session, when the participants and I were congratulating each other on what we all felt was a successful conclusion, the director said, "If this had been a real situation, you'd have all failed."

Four hours of effort and good feelings disappeared in a flash. The group turned sullen, packed their things, and left without another word to me or each other.

These are dicey issues. You don't want to risk alienating a senior manager or executive, who may have brought you in, but you don't want his or her opening or closing remarks to sabotage your hard-earned efforts. I believe you have to coach them (gently) by offering small reminders (or even provide a short paragraph or two) of how you'd like the person to open or close the training session.

9. Bad Closing Ceremonies by the Trainer

There is an art to starting a training program and an art to ending one. Begging for approval by begging for applause is cloying and creates discomfort in the audience. Ending too abruptly can create a tension in the group that gets reflected in the feedback sheets. Spend too long wrapping it up and people start leaving mid-sentence. The key to closing strongly is to use a combination of humility and a quick content review. Here's an approach that has worked for me:

> We've come to an end of our session and I want to tell you how much I've appreciated your participation and feedback. We've covered a lot of ground in a short period of time, including Topics A, B, C and Issues X, Y, Z. I hope I've given you some tools for success in these areas. And speaking of feedback, it's time to give me some, on the sheets we've provided for you. Thanks for coming. Please give yourself a hand for your hard work today. Thanks again.

The message here is simple: I'm asking you to clap for yourself, but in reality, you're clapping for us both. In a perfect world, your client or previous introducer will formally ask the crowd to give you a hand, but it's not a requirement. You're asking them to reward themselves for their efforts and, by proxy, your efforts as well. By giving a quick review of the core "Most Important Points," you give them a reminder of what to comment on, using the feedback sheets.

10. Bad Trainer

This is an obvious but painful one. Sometimes tough training topics are made even tougher by a lousy trainer. Everyone is entitled to a rough day, but some people in this business don't continuously improve or change their style, even when the feedback sheets and pointed comments from colleagues or the clients ask them to do so.

To survive in the training environment, you have to have some talent, some luck, and some guts. The best slides in the galaxy won't help if you can't connect with people. Teaching tough training topics is about building enough rapport to keep your group comfortable (they cannot learn much under stress), creating a safe learning environment so they can participate in the learning events, and imparting your knowledge in thoughtful, organized, and creative ways.

The Trainer's Mind

Getting Your Tools and Talents Ready to Teach

*Success in training adults is about
using two things: humor and stories.*

—Dr. Karl Albrecht

Key

Training is even tougher if you're not physically and psychologically ready to do it. This chapter discusses the need for you to sweat the little details and make sure the room design, the materials, the equipment, and your internal and external "self" are ready to put on a superior training performance.

In their book, *Presenting Magically,* neurolinguistic programming practitioners Dr. Tad James and David Shephard (2001) talk about having the "Trainer's Mind." Their concept says that if you really work to develop your state of mind as a professional trainer of people, prior to beginning every presentation, it will go a long way toward making a connection with those same people.

James and Shephard speak of "owning the stage" and creating congruence with the audience. They described some postures and poses that either build rapport or hurt it. Since we communicate more than half of our total messages via our body language, it's critical to understand how controlling your training "space" can put you on the road to success. And with tough training topics, you'll need every edge.

Creating Confidence: Setting the Stage for Success

Just after the O. J. Simpson criminal trial in 1995, I remember reading a book on the role and work of jury consultants. The writer (an attorney herself) captured an idea that holds true in the training world: Juries make up their minds about the legal participants (the judge, the attorneys, the defendant, and others) quite quickly, even before anyone has even opened his or her mouth. People, being what they are, make rapid value judgments, often incorrectly but "right" to them, based on initial reactions and intuitive feelings.

As such, the moment you walk into the room, you're on stage. Like an actor or actress in a movie, the people in that session will observe your every move, from the time you arrive and set down your briefcase to the moment you begin speaking. In their careful examination of you, the audience members are all looking for the answer to the same questions: Is this person going to waste my time? Is this person going to "enter-train" me? (Which is today's much-desired combination of entertainment and training, rolled into one presenter during each session.) Am I going to like this person? Will he or she call on me or do anything that will potentially embarrass me in front of my boss or peers?

Therefore, you must be as careful and methodical as possible, in front of the group, from the moment you enter the training room, until you begin the session. If you drop the handouts all over the floor, if you dump your coffee or water, or if you slam your briefcase, purse, or other personal items onto the table, it can reflect poorly on your subsequent skills as a trainer. It's human nature to accept the first impression as valid for the future.

Pre-Training (Outside the Room)

Here's an obvious but crucial point: Your audience will spend the next one to eight hours looking at you and listening to you. Your instruments for training are your voice and your body, so you've got to take care of both.

Gargle with Warm Salt Water a Few Hours Before You Begin. Make up a potion at the hotel or at home and give your pipes a good coating of saline. This has saved me many times, especially when doing back-to-back four-hour sessions and during cold/flu season.

Eat Lightly, Not Too Much Sugar. Stay away from the hotel cinnamon rolls and the doughnuts at the back of the training room, or your energy level will spike and then fall as your blood sugar dips about mid-morning or mid-afternoon.

Go Easy on the Coffee. While it has its medicinal qualities, it can also cause problems in your throat. If you find yourself clearing your throat a lot, it may be that your coffee is the culprit. The biggest concern from coffee, of course, is the caffeine. I'm a little edgy anyway, so I don't need the extra energy.

Hydrate After Every Hour Once You've Begun. Protecting your pipes starts and ends with drinking enough bottled water. Have an ample supply, even if you have to buy your own and lug it in.

Use the Restroom Long *Before* the Participants Get There. Remember that your ability to use the bathroom during breaks is often impeded by people who want to pepper you with questions. Sneak out during the video or exercise portions of the program.

Check Everything About Your Appearance Prior to the Start. Check your teeth, hair, and loose threads. Few things cut your credibility in half faster than a big food stain on the front of your clothing, a water stain on your pants, or the collar of your jacket or shirt sitting half up and half down. Little things like this can distract people into missing your message.

Upscale Your Clothes. I never believe the client when he or she says to me, "It's business casual, so you don't have to wear a tie." I do it anyway because you can always take it off (which can help as a rapport-building gesture with the group). Ladies and gentlemen who stand in front of people all day should look the part: well-tailored business suits, no loud jewelry, and appropriate accessories. There is an expectation of professionalism in our business. I don't wear my suit jacket longer than the first five minutes after the introduction, as

I like to make a small quip: "Now that you know that I own at least one good suit, I can take this off. Don't tell my mom."

You can also use clothing as a prop, to build rapport. I once taught a program on safety and security for a library in a small northern California town. My half-day program was part of a larger team-building session, which ran the entire workday and was given a Hawaiian theme. When I arrived, the whole library had been stylishly decorated with real palm trees, flowers, leis, and similar jungle-themed accoutrements.

All of the employees were dressed in Hawaiian shirts and khaki pants. After the library director introduced me, I thanked the group and told them I had to make a slight costume change. I took off my tie, unbuttoned my dress shirt, and while standing in my undershirt, tossed them onto the floor with a flourish. I removed my favorite Hawaiian shirt from my briefcase and slipped it on. I said, "Okay. Now I'm really ready." They clapped and cheered for two minutes. Small gesture, big result.

Recheck Your Handouts and Slides. In most cases, you will provide them or the client will. There is room for error in either case. If you can check them the night before, so much the better. If not, get them from the client early enough to see if there are any errors you have to adjust for on the fly. Check your slides one more time as well, even if it's a program you've done before. Software plays tricks on us.

Recheck Your Equipment. Another benefit of getting there early is to make sure your laptop, the projector (yours or theirs), the VCR/TV, the easel pads, and the room seating arrangement are all set.

Practice Stress Breathing. If you're under a lot of pre-training stress, practice four-way breathing. This technique is similar to what they teach soldiers in combat. Shallow breathing is bad for the pulse rate and cognitive skills. Too much or not enough respiration makes you feel lightheaded. If you start to feel this way, try the following four-way breathing technique:

- At your own pace, inhale slowly to the count of four.

- Hold it for a count of four.

- Exhale slowly to a count of four.

- Repeat this until you've done it four times.

Pre-Training (Inside the Room)

Use Music to Calm the Savage Breast

I'm surprised how infrequently I see other trainers use music as a part of their pre-training rituals. Since most laptops have either Windows Media Player® or the Apple Macintosh® version pre-loaded on them, it's easy and fast to simply place some pleasant, non-competitive music (no lyrics, no pulsing rock beats, just relaxing sounds) onto your Playlist. When you play music behind your title slide, you can create a significant change in both the perspective and the expectations of the arriving group. As they mill about the coffee area or find their seats, the presence of music sends a signal that says it's time for them to shift their focus to something and someone new.

Your local music store (and bookstore) probably have a selection of music that is low-key, relaxing, and appropriate for every audience. (*Note:* Be sure to obtain permission from the copyright holder to use music during a session. Copyright-free and royalty-free music is available at www.trainers warehouse.com.)

The key is not to play the music loud enough to compete with pre-training conversations nor draw attention to itself as a distraction. It simply sits in the background and helps to create an atmosphere more conducive to learning.

Some trainers use software programs that display a series of ever-changing pictures on the screen, related to nature scenes, animals, fish, people, and so forth. If you're using Windows Media Player®, you can display the pre-installed visualizations in the background of the music as well.

Set the Mood with Lighting

Adjust the lighting so it does not shine directly on the screen. If it's possible, lower the room lights in general. You want to create a mood, an impression that something special is going to happen, not just another training program in a brightly lit cavern, taught by some man or some woman in a nice suit, armed with a PowerPoint® projector and an easel pad.

Post the Courtesy List Poster

The Courtesy List comes from my California training colleague, Jim Vidakovich, author of *Trainers in Motion.* Since Jim's background is in television, he knows training is a visual medium. You can post the Courtesy List as either an easel pad page, tacked on a nearby wall, where the maximum number of people can see it, or you can create a simple slide and use it as a pre-training reminder on the screen. Here are some points for the Courtesy List:

- Please practice "digital courtesy" by putting all cell phones and pagers on silent mode.

- Please come back from breaks and lunches on time.

- Please avoid side conversations during the training.

- Please respect each other and each contribution.

Greet People as They Arrive

Depending on the nature of the program and the subject you're going to be covering, go into a meet-and-greet mode with as many participants as you can contact before you formally begin. Demonstrate your humanity, sense of humor, and desire to connect with them even before the program begins. I believe the tougher the training topic, the more you have to bridge the distance between you (the perceived subject expert) and the audience (the recipients of your knowledge) who may feel more than a bit apprehensive about what you may have them say or do.

Keep remembering that most people have a natural disinclination to participate in front of their peers. It's common for people filing in to make a concerted effort not to sit anywhere near the front row, for fear you'll call on them, joke with or tease them, or otherwise create some embarrassing scene for them in front of their colleagues.

I've lost count of the number of times I've been preparing to teach my workplace violence prevention program and heard a couple of attendees snicker in my direction and say, "Ha! Ha! This guy's gonna teach us how to be violent! Ha Ha!"

As you can imagine, the first three hundred times it was funny. I simply smile politely and go about my business. Know that you'll hear variations on the same theme for other tough topics: "This woman's gonna teach us how to sexually harass people!" or "This class is about how to use drugs and alcohol," and so forth, until you have a regular laugh riot on your hands. Keep in mind that some people use (ill-timed) humor as their own peculiar antidote for stress.

Once the program has begun, besides giving the "Low-Stress Learning Speech" (described below), I have often pulled out a wad of dollar bills and peeled one off for each person who I say "had the courage" to sit in the front row. This usually creates much laughter and relief, as everyone realizes: (a) I have a sense of humor and (b) I'm not going to put anyone on the spot.

Pre-Training Posture

As I discussed in the section on Creating Confidence, your moves prior to the start of the session must be precise and deliberate, to further convey the message that you are a polished, prepared professional. Always keep in mind that nothing in that description says that you have to be serious, even if you're teaching serious subjects.

One example of how trainers can fall victim to the toughness of their topics is the "Stone-Face Syndrome." Here, they have wrongly let the gravity of their subjects take over and they become afflicted with the inability to smile, joke around a bit, or build early rapport. To fall victim to this disease you simply stop smiling, adapt a visage that puts out a "stay away" signal, and continue your pre-training preparations. People will avoid you, brief and pleasant conversations will disappear, and you will find yourself wondering why the feedback sheets may use labels like "intense" or "unapproachable" to describe you.

Rationalizations for this façade abound: "We have to act this way," say the Stone-Facers, "otherwise people will think we're weak, unfocused, or not serious."

The antidote to this disease is simpler than you might expect: smile more. The late and great Dale Carnegie advised that you always keep what he called "an emerging smile on your face," no matter what the circumstances. Just changing your posture from slumped shoulders to a more upright stance, and from a sour puss to the edge of a smile *can* suddenly change the way you feel.

Imagine your expression when you walk around after you've just heard a piece of really great news. That's the Dale Carnegie look in action. It's not about convincing the world you're tough; it's about convincing the world you're not tough *all the time.*

Greeting people with social pleasantries, smiles, and a lighter touch, even and especially when you're all facing a tough training topic, helps begin to break down the natural resistance they feel coming in the training room.

During the Session
Your Stance During the Introduction

First, you should *never* allow people to wing it when it comes to introducing you. Even if you are an internal trainer and the head of HR is introducing you to employees you both already know, there is still a stage to be set by the use of the bio sheet. Which of these two examples sets the stage for your success?

HR Director: "Hey, everybody, listen up. Here's Mary to get us started with her time management stuff." (points to you and then wanders away)
or

HR Director: "Good morning, everyone. We all know Mary, from our Training Division. She's asked me to talk about why you're here today. (Reads from your sheet.) Our goal is to help you manage your time, both personally and professionally, so that you feel like you can get your projects done in a way that best balances your work and home life. So, she's ready and I know you'll want to hear what she has to say about this important topic."

It's important for everyone associated with launching the training program (you, the introducer, the audiovisual crews, and others) to do what they can to set the stage for your success. Since they won't always know how to do this, you have to give them gentle but direct guidance. One way is to provide the introductory comments and your bio sheet for them, so they don't have to stress themselves over what to say. Keep in mind that some of these folks may not relish standing in front of employees, peers, or their bosses either, so you should help them kick off the event using a structured, written format, like we see in the second example above.

Now for an interesting issue: How do you stand—literally—when the person introducing you is reading the bio sheet you created? Do you look proud, haughty even, while someone reveals your educational, organizational, or business accomplishments? Do you look at the audience or the introducer? Do you try the "aw shucks" approach and appear to look away in bemused detachment? Once again the answer is: It depends.

My preference is to stay slightly off-center from the front of the room, about ten feet from the person introducing me. This is not a game show, so I don't like to wait behind the group as I'm being introduced. Having them crane their necks in circles as they look for me is distracting to us all. I smile slightly at the group and switch my gaze from them to my introducer.

(I have a unique bio—I'm a retired police sergeant, among other career paths and accomplishments—so when I hear the police portion of my bio during my safety, security, and workplace violence programs, I look straight at the introducer because I can always feel the crowd's eyes all shift to me at that point. It's like they suddenly see me in a new light and the pressure is palpable.)

When teaching tough training topics, I believe overt shyness about your status as a trainer is the wrong approach. You *want* them to think you are the best at what you do and frankly, you are the *best choice* of all the people in the world they could have selected to come here and teach this particular program. You want your bio and the person reading it to project a sense of both subject-matter competence and training skill.

Three or four paragraphs (double-spaced) are more than sufficient to make your case. Be bold and a bit unique in your bio/intro. Don't start with your name first; start with a significant accomplishment. Embed your name after an opening statement that's illustrative, humorous, or even provocative. Some examples:

- "In 2005, our presenter wrote the first book in the U.S. on Issue X. He's going to tell us what that experience taught him about Issue Y."

- "Our presenter today believes that training is more about you teaching her than her lecturing to you. She's here to explain what she means."

- "Your trainer today earned his doctoral degree in less than three years. He will explain how that ruined his ability to read a book without highlighting the testable material."

- "Last year, our trainer presented this session to a delegation of Chinese business people in Beijing."

I always use the ending phrase, "Please help me welcome Dr. Steve Albrecht," not because I'm trolling for applause, but because it signals the formal beginning of the program in a way that's structured and not haphazard, like saying, "Here he is."

I also use the ending of the introduction as my first attempts at humor, to gauge the mood of the crowd. Some examples:

- "Thank you. Please retake your seats. Please sit down, you're embarrassing me."

- "Good morning. My mom gets a royalty check each time someone reads that bio she wrote for me."

- "Thank you for having me. After that long list of accomplishments, I bet many of you were expecting a much older man would stand up."

- "Good morning. How many people here were so excited about this topic that you couldn't wait to get here? Did anybody sleep outside so you could be first in line?"

If I get a particularly robust round of opening applause and I have bantered with the group a bit before we began so I know they're in a good mood, I often steal this line from David Letterman: "Thanks very much for that warm welcome. [PAUSE] However, I'm still going to go ahead with the program."

The point is that many people sleep through the introduction of the trainer because of all the usual and boring platitudes, for example, "Sue was born at a very young age . . ." or "Pete barely gets his feet wet when he walks on the water. . . ."

The more you can shake up this tired format, the more attention participants will pay, because it sends an early message: This is going to be different, not what you thought, and better than you expected.

Making the "Low-Stress Learning" Speech: Give the Crowd a Breather

There are certain training subjects that are just more fun to attend. The facilitator makes you feel comfortable because the subject is comfortable. As a result of good rapport building with the crowd, the facilitator can get the group to do almost anything, from performing a skit to singing a song together.

Alas, I don't usually have the luxury of a non-threatening or easier-than-most topic to teach. I also completely lack the ability or desire to take the group down that particular path. I do not have the capacity to subject myself to a high-stress approach, via my own ego death. Some of my best friends in the training community have such confidence in themselves and their abilities that they will put on clown noses, break into funny accents, and cavort around the room. The group likes them, buys into this particular concept for training people, and they get away with it every time.

My rationalization is that my personality style borders on the intense; I'm as task focused as can be and I can't bear to be purposely embarrassed while on the training platform. Perhaps this stems from the paradox of my profession: I'm an introvert trapped in an extrovert's job. I deeply enjoy the training process, I like being in front of people, and my ego is strong enough to be able to engage with any group or any person, on any issue, at any time.

However, when I'm done for the day, I'm really done. Unlike the extrovert trainer, who feeds off the group and often finishes with as much or more energy as when he or she started, I'm spent. I don't have the personality type, the energy, or the tools necessary to subject the group and myself to lots of "outside the box" training techniques. You can't fake this training style. You either have the ego to use these high-energy, high-involvement approaches to get adults to learn, or you do not. I do not.

As such, while my programs tend to be High Content—High Delivery, I use an approach driven by stories, humor, and a Socratic questioning style,

which engages heavily with a lot of the audience members as I go. I rationalize this approach (which is far away from some of the "fun" group exercises
involving paper hats, drinking straws, and mini-staplers) as the one that fits
my personality and keeps me in my training comfort zone.

I also believe (or rationalize) that as adults grow older, they wish to risk less.
Consider the following passage written by John Gardner, the former Health,
Education, and Welfare Secretary, founder of Common Cause, and a leader in
the civil rights era under President Lyndon B. Johnson. In his 1964 book *Self-
Renewal: The Individual and the Innovative Society,* Gardner writes of the need
for people to take chances in their lives, to break old habits, to see things in new
ways instead of always relying on what's certain and comfortable:

> As we mature we progressively narrow the scope and variety of our
> lives. Of all the interests we might pursue, we settle on a few. Of all
> the people with whom we might associate, we select a small number.
> We become caught in a web of fixed relationships. We develop set
> ways of doing things.
>
> As the years go by we view our familiar surroundings with less
> and less freshness of perception. We no longer look with a wakeful,
> perceiving eye at the faces of people we see every day, nor at any other
> features of our everyday world.
>
> It is not unusual to find that the major changes in life—a marriage,
> a move to a new city, a change of jobs, or a national emergency—break
> the patterns of our lives and reveal to us quite suddenly how much we
> had been imprisoned by the comfortable web we had woven around
> ourselves.
>
> One of the reasons why mature people are apt to learn less than
> young people is that they are willing to risk less. Learning is a risky
> business, and they do not like failure. In infancy, when the child is
> learning at a truly phenomenal rate—a rate he or she will never again
> achieve—he or she is also experiencing a shattering number of failures.
> Watch him or her. See the innumerable things he or she tries and fails.
> And see how little the failures discourage him or her.

With each year that passes he or she will be less blithe about failure. By adolescence the willingness of young people to risk failure has diminished greatly. And all too often parents push them further along that road by instilling fear, by punishing failure, or by making success seem too precious.

By middle age most of us carry around in our heads a tremendous catalogue of things we have no intention of trying again because we tried them once and failed—or tried them once and did less well than our self-esteem demanded.

By middle life, most of us are *accomplished fugitives* [emphasis mine] from ourselves.

Put this into a training perspective, and it's hard to read this passage and not consider our own lives as examples of the power of the fear of failure, so much that we don't ever try anything new or interesting. It's also hard to read this passage and not shudder at the phrase "accomplished fugitives," for it paints a painful picture of how avoiding risk and falling into the same dull routines affects us all.

I believe many adults, who come to training programs either by choice or by mandate, have become part of Gardner's accomplished fugitives when it comes to taking risks with their learning. Therefore, even though it goes against the new era of interactive, purpose-driven, "enter-trainment," I tell my participants right from the start that there will be no funny hats, skits, songs, or ways to ridicule me or themselves through drawing, dancing, or standing on chairs. "Relax," I tell them, "I won't give us any opportunities to suffer humiliation, teasing, or ego death during this training session."

I say, "I will use and look for low-stress opportunities to engage with you all as the group, without putting either of us at risk of embarrassment. None of this means we won't have fun, because I plan on having fun. This is a tough subject in other people's eyes, but I like it and I like you, so we will succeed together."

After I've made this announcement, you can hear many people in the audience sighing audibly and blinking noticeably as they look around at each other with obvious relief.

Going to Breaks, Returning from Breaks

Consider some "Why it's time to take a break" factoids:

- The human brain tends to cycle on and off, in terms of its comprehension span, about every 90 minutes. Too much forced concentration, after that time period, tends to stifle further comprehension.

- The average one-pack per day smoker can go about 20 minutes without starting to feel the psychological or physiological effects of wanting another cigarette.

- Participants who drink coffee, tea, sodas, or water in the morning will need more breaks than those who drink these liquids in the afternoon. Why? More food in their stomachs later slows the movement to the bladder.

- Too many breaks interrupt the flow and make many people feel like they're not getting very much content out of the training experience. Too few breaks makes many people feel edgy or anxious (full bladders, missed cell phone messages, too much focus on content and not enough on delivery).

- Participants tend to come back right on time from breaks that take place at odd times: 9:13 A.M. to 9:23 A.M. or 12:11 P.M. to 1:11 P.M.

I have seen trainers lose rapport with their groups because of the way they handled the break situation. You must take the pulse of the crowd frequently enough to know when they need a break.

In a three- to four-hour program, make the first break the longest. For full-day programs in crowded business areas, consider early lunch breaks (11:30) or late ones (12:30) so that the audience can get a full hour to eat their lunches.

I foreshadow my breaks, so the participants will know I haven't forgotten them or their need for a break, for example, "We'll be taking a break very, very soon" and then later, "Right after this slide, we'll take 15 minutes," then, "We're going to break now. See you back in your seats and ready to go at 10:19."

Trainers can also lose control of the crowd when the break period is over, when people are milling about, instead of sitting back down. Here, you have to raise your voice loud enough to be heard over the din of coffee and conversation, "We're about to get started," and then when nearly everyone is back in, "Welcome back, everybody. Thanks for coming back on time. I'd like to start again by focusing on. . . ." For larger groups in larger rooms, I don't wait for every single soul to get seated; I use the power of peer pressure (I start talking, right on time—recall the Courtesy List criteria) to get them quiet and ready to go on.

Closing Comments

Just as you can lose the group at the introduction or by mismanaging the breaks, you can also lose them by mangling the closing. A strong close not only helps to reinforce what you just spent several hours or days talking about, but it also warms them to an important task: giving you good feedback.

Here's what I often say to get two birds with the same stone:

> We've come to an important part of this training session—the end. I know some of you are sad to see me go and others are glad I've run out of things to say. I've appreciated your feedback and support as I've taught this program. I know it's hard to stay focused on my words when you have so many other issues facing you at home or at work. I appreciate your attention as well. It's a privilege for me to do this work, and I do it for one reason: so you can take some of the things we've talked about here, like Issues X, Y, and Z, and put them to good use, starting today. We are all here to take care of ourselves and each other. Thanks for taking care of me. Please take a moment to fill out the feedback sheet you were given at the start of this program. Remember "certified genius" is spelled with one "s." Seriously, you've made it easy for me to do a good job for you. Please give yourselves a round of applause, as I will do for you too. Take care and thanks. We're adjourned."

The Perfect Training Experience

The following list speaks for itself. Here's what makes this part of your career worthwhile. When your training engine is clicking on all cylinders, it's a beautiful thing:

- You arrive on time.

- There are no audio issues.

- The lighting does not glare on the screen.

- Every piece of electronic equipment works.

- The videos are cued up perfectly and play flawlessly.

- The color of the slides is perfect for the lighting in the room.

- The crowd arrives on time.

- You start on time.

- The introducer reads your bio sheet perfectly.

- There is bottled water and an extra table for your materials.

- The audience's seats are not too hard or too soft.

- The room is not too hot or too cold.

- The handouts are there, with no smudges, and no missing or backwards pages.

- There are no pillars or obstructed views.

- You don't have to compete with any inside or outside-the-room noises.

- The group is lively, energetic, and responsive to you and your material.

- The group follows your instructions and completes each individual or group exercise.

- The group comes back from breaks on time.

- You finish on time.

- The group gives you appropriate and respectful feedback and praise.

Future Pacing: Visualize Your Way to Success

If you're not just a bit nervous before an important training program, something is definitely wrong. Even the longtime presenter pros have a short case of the butterflies-in-the-stomach, even if they have been doing the same program for more than a long while. The same holds true for actors and actresses, working on stage or on film, who feel the tension of their pending performance, even if it's one they're comfortable with.

Keep in mind that other people may be nervous for you as well. To the internal or external client, who brought you in front of the group in the first place, *every* training session is important; their reputation is attached to your success too. They don't want to have to hear from the feedback sheets or worse, their boss(es): "Who brought this whiz kid in here? He or she was awful! Let's do a better job next time with the company money and people. Let's make sure we pick someone who knows our business, knows this topic, and who has the proven experience to do this thing right."

As such, a little pre-show tension is helpful; too much is debilitating. Even veteran trainers get tense before a program, where one or more elements help to add to the pressure. But whether your stress is caused by bad lighting, bad snacks in the back of the room, or a terrible introduction by your host, you have to press on and do a more than commendable job.

The clients do not really care about your pounding headache; the blister on your right foot; the fight you had the night before with your boss, spouse, or kids; your lousy plane flight; or any other outside concern of yours. They may be politely interested in these problems of yours, but not to the degree where they will use them as an appropriate justification if you don't perform well in front of their people. It's a hard world; you may get credit for doing a great job under trying circumstances: a taxicab crash on the way over, a power outage that strikes mid-program, or a diabolically evil heckler in the crowd. You won't get a free pass on any of these fronts if you don't perform well.

So how can you assure yourself of training success, even before you ever step in front of the group? It may help to practice a form of visualization-for-success called *future pacing*. It's neither man-bites-dog in terms of its novelty or newness, nor is it mental voodoo. It's simply a structured method to help you get your Trainer's Mind in sync with your Trainer's Body. And if it's good enough for Tiger Woods, Michael Jordan, and countless other professional athletes, then it's good enough for us as well.

Put simply, future pacing is a focused relaxation exercise that helps you visualize your successful performance in a forthcoming, potentially stressful event. It's a self-directed, self-guided process that helps you "see" success and exceptional performance in your mind, long before you have to actually do it. Let's say you have to fly to another city, stay overnight, and teach a new program to a new client the next day. Here are the steps for future pacing:

1. Find a safe place where you can spend about 20 minutes of un-interrupted, quiet time, sitting comfortably, with your eyes closed. (This removes driving in your car as one of the locations to use future pacing.)

2. With your eyes closed, start to visualize your next training assignment, starting with the process to get in front of the group and ending with the first 10 minutes of your session with them.

3. In your mind's eye, visualize all of the little details and hear yourself walk through them, comfortably, successfully, and without stress: "Here I am packing my clothes, materials, and equipment. Here I am driving to the airport. Now I'm getting my boarding pass and going through security. Here I am on the plane. Now I see myself going to the hotel. Here I am in my hotel room, preparing myself and my materials for the next day. Here I am getting a comfortable and peaceful night of good sleep."

4. See every little detail of the next day, when you'll be conducting the training program. Take your mind through each of the encounters until the moment you begin to speak to the group: "Here I am driving to the location. I can see that I have all my equipment and I'm ready to meet the client. Here I am shaking hands with the client and looking at the training room. Now I'm setting up my equipment with no problems at all. I'm starting to greet the participants as they arrive. Now I'm listening to the person who will introduce me as he or she reads my bio sheet. I can hear the group applauding for me as I step to the front of the room. Here I am shaking hands with the person who introduced me. Here is the first thing I'm going to say to the group, now the second, and now the third . . ." At this point, you should be rolling and into the meat of your training program.

Future pacing is all about convincing your mind and your body that you're experiencing some déjà vu. If you practice this process successfully (and it's hard not to do it correctly the very first time you try it), when you get to the day in question—the flight, the hotel, the training room, and so forth—you will hear yourself saying, "This looks familiar. This feels familiar. This sounds familiar, almost as if I've already done this." Getting into that "been here, done that" mindset is very calming because we find comfort in our routines.

I've been practicing this exact same technique for nearly two decades. It works best for those stress-filled encounters where the fear of the unknown (Will I succeed? Will my equipment work? Will they like me?) gets in the way of your natural abilities and hard-earned talents. It may not be necessary to use this technique for every training program, just the ones that you know are becoming a stressor or a distraction.

Whether you call it self-hypnosis, guided imagery, or pre-visualization, practicing the art of future pacing can help allay your pre-training jitters better and more ethically than a shot of bourbon. Try it for the next thirty days and see whether you don't start feeling more comfortable about your pending programs.

3

Tough Topics and Tough Crowds

You don't have to like it, you just have to do it.

—Commander Richard Marcinko, USN,
Leadership Secrets of the Rogue Warrior

Key

We define tough crowds and tough participants as any audience member who challenges your right to be in front of the group; gripes about the length, content, or need for the training; or simply makes it hard for others to learn by being rude, inconsiderate, or hostile.

When comedian George Carlin speaks of his early days in comedy, he says he really got his start back in the school classroom. This "comedy training ground" provided him with endless opportunities to be the Class Clown. "Well," he would say to himself, before launching into another series of antics in the classroom, "why not deprive someone else of their education?"

Disruptive participants are different from participants who simply lack social intelligence. Disruptive people often have a hidden agenda and *want* to draw attention to themselves or their complaints and concerns. People who lack social intelligence (defined as the capacity to realize that your behavior impacts other people) may not seek out attention, but they can draw others into their world, based on their irritating behavior. My distinction between these two categories of tough crowd members is important because it affects our discussion of how to manage them during the training session.

Learning Styles
Generational Issues

> *Change the learning method every 20 minutes.*
>
> —Bob Pike, from his Creative Training Techniques seminar

Before we examine the behaviors of our toughest critics, it may help to heighten our understanding of how adults learn. Much has been written in the popular media about the learning styles and differences between the so-called Baby Boom Generation (born 1946–1964), Generation X (born 1965–1979), and Generation Y (born 1980–1994). There are plenty of theories we can apply to adult-based training for each of these social segments. I'm going to make some sweeping generalizations about all of these groups, without getting bogged down in too much detail.

Based on what we know about experiential learning versus lecture-based learning, we can posit that the younger age groups

- *Tend to learn best by doing, rather than via straight lecture.* They are increasingly more comfortable with group exercises because more of the emphasis in their work cultures is on team-based work, group projects, brainstorming meetings, team-building exercises, and similar methods.

- *Tend to like visual stimulation in the training environment* (Hollywood-quality training videos, music, arousing or futuristic color schemes in the slides).

- *Want to be asked for their opinions during the training,* through Q&A sessions, on-the-spot polls or surveys, and open discussions with time and space for feedback from the presenter and the rest of the group.

- *Tend to be easily distracted* by the quickening pace of our culture (lots of situations and events pull them away from a more complete focus on the training subjects).

- *Tend to be very comfortable with expanding technology.* Gen X and Y are very familiar with new cell phone features, PDAs, pagers, digital cameras, laptops, constant e-mail access, and creating and manipulating video and audio clips, MP3 players, and so on. As such, they have an expectation that the trainer will incorporate these different media into the training program.

Neurolinguistic Programming

Aficionados of the concept of neurolinguistic programming, or NLP, suggest that there are three types of learners in any training audience. While there are no absolute certainties when it comes to how people take in and process information, we can focus on some general conclusions for each, widely known in the NLP parlance as auditory, visual, and kinesthetic learners.

Auditory Learners. These people tend to learn best while hearing someone describe a concept or idea. They have a good memory for spoken-word details. If a stranger were to give them directions in a strange town, they could drive right to the spot without writing down the myriad of left and right turns. Auditory learners tend to like lecture formats more than other styles, especially when the presenter changes his or her vocal pace, pitch, and tone with some regularity. They can hear and interpret complex stories or instructions more readily than those with other styles. They can "tune in" and "tune out" of a conversation or a training exercise, just by listening or not listening on demand. When training for people with this preference, you may want to use language that emphasizes *sounds*: "How does that sound to you?" or "Let me repeat back what I think I'm hearing from you or the group."

Visual Learners. This type of learner seems to respond best to visual stimuli. They tend to appreciate a visual-based use of language, for example, videos, colorful slides, photos, maps, diagrams, charts, etc. Visual thinkers tend to like "visual movement," which is why they are comfortable interpreting data and imagery from television, movies, and computer screens (games, business-specific software like PowerPoint™ slides, and other color-driven programs). Static displays of information tend to put their feet to sleep. When training for them, change the learning modality frequently by changing what they see around them (even altering the lighting may give them a new "view" of something in the room) and incorporate more color into your slides, handouts, and easel pad exercises.

They tend to "paint word pictures" and are most comfortable when you use a *visual* vocabulary: "How do you see it?" or "Am I making myself clear enough as I give you a snapshot of the exercise?" or "Here's what I picture when I see this part unfold."

Kinesthetic (or "Haptic") Learners. Whereas the auditory learner would probably ask someone to explain how to use a new piece of software, and the visual learner would probably go to the on-screen tutorial (complete with video clips) to learn it best, the hands-on learner (also known as kinesthetic or haptic) would probably want to sit down at the computer screen, grab the mouse, and begin figuring it out for himself or herself. These folks tend to not wait for every piece of data (reading the entire software manual, sitting through an entire class that was not hands-on) before they take a crack at something, even if it's highly complex or technical. They often fly by the seat of their pants, comfortable with their experience, a wealth of common sense, mechanical skills, and past successes in learning by doing.

The key to working with kinesthetic learners is your ability to give them an early chance to succeed with whatever you're teaching them. Get them involved in the course notebook quickly, start with an exercise right after your introduction, or get them up and moving around the room with a table-team assignment. Stay away from abstract discussions, and instead use words that emphasize *"feeling"* the issue: "Tell me how you feel about the concept?" or "What's your gut reaction to it?" or "How do you plan to get a handle on this project?"

The $64,000 question for all this, of course, is, "How do I identify which style I'm dealing with in the training environment?" The short answer is that every person carries some portion of each of these learning styles around with him or her, so it helps to provide material, exercises, or lecture formats that appeal to all three. The longer answer is that most people tend to have a *dominant* style, which is their learning style preference.

Many people who have careers in the training world have a solid understanding of the NLP theories. They've read about them or have seen them demonstrated in the training environment before. If you'd like more information on NLP theory and operational use in the training room, then you'll need to do a bit of research. There are a number of good books on NLP and several leading NLP practitioners, including Dr. Tad James, David Shephard, Dr. Wil Horton, and others, who offer courses and deeper instruction.

Cognitive Styles

My father, Dr. Karl Albrecht, has pioneered his own instrument, based on cognitive styles, which he calls "Mindex." The Mindex instrument makes distinctions for thinking styles by focusing on the hemispheric differences between left-brained thinkers and right-brained thinkers.

As a review, left-brained thinkers tend to be more focused on data, processing information, and structures. They are comfortable using models, theories, diagrams, plans, and concepts. They tend to take jobs where this style is appreciated: computers, science, medicine, engineering, accounting, project planning, data interpretation, and data management.

Right-brained thinkers tend to be more focused on feelings, intuition, commonsense approaches, and emotions. They tend to take jobs where creativity and the human interaction is prevalent: nursing, teaching, managing people over projects, sales, marketing, advertising, counseling, and work where more artistic over mechanistic design is required.

Mindex connects the two concepts of left- and right-brained thinkers with the idea that there are people who tend toward more concrete thinking and others who tend toward more abstract thinking. As such, Karl has devised four metaphorical cognitive styles:

- Blue Earth—Left-Brained, Concrete Thinkers

- Red Earth—Right-Brained, Concrete Thinkers

- Blue Sky—Left-Brained, Abstract Thinkers

- Red Sky—Right-Brained, Abstract Thinkers

And while people can dwell in any of the four areas as necessary, statistically speaking (as the Mindex norm base of users has suggested), most people tend to have a favorite or dominant style. Keeping in mind that all of us move through all four styles, and that no one style is more superior to any other, it helps to orient your training designs toward the needs of all four types.

Blue Earth Thinkers are comfortable with accurate data, numbers, facts and figures, and word problems. They like working with case studies or issues where the answer is qualitative and precise. "About four or so" doesn't do it for them. They tend to like "bottom-line" results and often speak in these terms. They tend to dislike exercises that are too humanistic, or what they would perceive as too touchy-feely.

Red Earth Thinkers are comfortable with people. They like to engage with others and often use their initial intuitive, gut feelings to make decisions about people, projects, or problems. Too much data and way too much theory tends to scare them away from complex training exercises. They are hands-on learners, who like to connect with others and solve problems in creative, outside-the-box ways.

Blue Sky Thinkers are comfortable with models, theories, grids, charts, project plans, and other ideas that can be characterized best visually, on paper, or through a careful explanation by a subject-matter expert. They tend to draw sketches and models when describing things to others, ironically, not so much for other people's benefits, but for their own organizational needs. They tend not to need to make a social connection in the training environment, and often prefer to work alone or at their own pace on projects or exercises.

Red Sky Thinkers are comfortable being an "idea machine." They tend to be highly imaginative, creative thinkers, who can see the world of possibilities when asked for solutions. They are great brainstormers and can think divergently for a long period of time. As such, they tend not to be comfortable with highly convergent exercises, where time is short and only one answer will solve the presenting problem.

There are, of course, no absolutes when it comes to the thinking styles, cognitive abilities, and learning dynamics of your participants. The more tools you can have in your training tool kit, the easier it will be for you to make changes or respond differently to their learning needs once you've discovered their most likely learning preferences.

Comfort Zones

In a seminar-style program, where you have a limited time and/or a smaller and more manageable group of employees or supervisors, it helps sometimes to design your program so you can hit the following three types of learners almost immediately.

"Let's Get to It" Learners. These folks are happiest when something is happening. They want to roll up their sleeves (literally) and get going. For them, time spent on lengthy introductions, agenda discussions, or too much theory is a big waste. They want to either dive into the course notebook or handouts or get involved in some activity that stimulates them.

You can get some clues as to the presence of these types by their pre-training behavior. While others may be sitting quietly, getting coffee, or otherwise milling about, they have already opened the course notebook or cracked open the handouts. Before the program begins, they have already read your bio sheet, scanned the overall content design of the manual, and may have even begun to do some of the exercises or self-assessment tools.

If I see I have several of this type, one of the things I will do as a conversation starter, right after I introduce myself, is say: "If you're wearing a wrist watch today, please cover it with your hand. Now, without looking at it, turn to the person right next to you and describe the face of your watch in rich detail. Ready, set, go!"

This usually starts the group buzzing a bit and most people who have a watch play along with each other. I let this run for about three minutes and then I say, "Okay, stop! Now uncover your watch and see what you might have missed."

By now, they're all laughing at themselves because almost no one ever describes his or her own wrist watch accurately. I get them back together by saying this, "For many things in life and work, little details are surprisingly important. We are going to spend some time today looking at the big picture, some macro themes around this training topic. But we are also going to look closely at some micro issues—the small things, the little details—that can help you understand this topic more completely. Let's begin."

So what have I done so far? I've broken the ice, forced people to engage with each other, and already given the "Let's Get to It" learner something to do.

"Let's Meet Everyone First" Learners. These folks are people-people; they enjoy seeing old friends and relish the chance to make new ones. They are often social, vibrant, extroverted, and interested in having a good time while they learn some things.

I can spot them by their pre-training behavior as well. They hug old friends, introduce themselves to me and the people around them, and generally send off a signal that says, "I'm approachable."

For these people, I play the "Name Game," which always seems to get the group off to a good start. The Name Game uses a bit of peer pressure, mixed with a little touch of performance anxiety, to teach the group to pay attention, focus on their colleagues, and remember their names for later. Here's how to play it:

Let's say there are twenty people in the training group. I start by asking them to remove their name tags or cover their desktop name plates (if applicable). Then I tell them, "I will go around the room and when I come to you, please point to yourself and just tell us your first name. The person next to you will then repeat your name and add his or her name next."

When we start, the group soon realizes that the deeper I go into the crowd, the more names they will suddenly have to remember! The first person points to himself and says, "Dave." The next person points to herself and says, "Dave, Mary." Then Mary's colleague has to point to himself and say, "Dave, Mary, Pete," and so on until the last person has to repeat back every name he or she has heard, plus add his or her own. I will take the anchor position and repeat every name in the room, and then add my own. It always amazes me how this icebreaker gets plenty of laughs and builds cohesion so quickly. We have fun with it, adding in a bit of teasing for the mistakes, and it forces the last people to really focus on the names and concentrate in front of their peers. It satisfies those with a need to "do something" as part of the training, and the "Let's Meet Everyone First" people love it.

"Leave Me Alone" Learners. These are the toughest of the three. They have come to learn (or not) and they don't want to talk to anyone. (Full disclosure: As an introvert trapped in an extrovert's job, I find myself in this category when I attend small-setting training programs put on by other people. If I don't know a soul in the room, I often just sit and look at the materials, rather than network or socialize. My rationalization is similar to the notion that the shoemaker's kids have bad shoes: I do this for a living, so it's hard for me to engage with total strangers if I just did it all day yesterday. Sometimes, I tell myself, I need a break from people and I just want to focus on my own learning.)

The distinction with these learners is a fine one; they may not intend to be rude, but their passivity and "stay-away" non-verbal message can give others this impression. Some trainers take the approach that they should force these people out of their shells, using exercises or games where they have to be the leader or facilitator. I have found this to be counter-productive in most training settings. While shy people are often quite bright and engaging when given an opportunity that keeps them in their comfort zone, they don't always relish grabbing the marking pen and stepping up to the easel pad, like the previous two learner types.

For these people, I use two techniques: spokesperson rotations and looping back. For the former, I use enough table-team exercises so that everyone at the table has to take the lead position at least once during the program. I say, "Will the last spokesperson from your group please pick a new facilitator for this next exercise? Please choose someone who hasn't been a facilitator before." This gets even the quiet ones involved, in a low-stress way. (It has an added benefit of keeping the attention hogs from moving to the front and taking over every exercise. This is especially a problem in very passive groups, who will often allow the dominant member to do everything for them.)

Looping back suggests that I try to engage with different people at each of the table teams, by name, every few minutes. I just pick different people to call on for public feedback or comments, so that no one goes unnoticed or can sit through the whole session without making at least a few remarks. I try to do this in a low-key way, not calling on them in a demanding tone, like I was some kind of mean old headmaster, but by using polite questioning: "Jane, what are your thoughts on this issue?" or "Jeff, please tell us your perspective on this."

All of this supports a training style for all three that moves away from straight lecture and more toward constant interactivity with the participants. Using these techniques, along with your own collection of stories, humor, video, games, exercises, and even magic tricks, you can engage with all three learning styles at once.

Special Category Audiences

The concept of alignment in training suggests that we are always trying for the best fit between the trainer, the materials, and the audience. If you have two out of the three, you can survive a tough training topic relatively well. Only one out of the three makes it more difficult, and having none out of the three makes it nearly impossible to have a good performance.

In terms of certain subsets of participant groups, some have developed a reputation for being tough critics and hard audiences. I have seen members of more than one of the following groups send novice trainers running from the room in near-tears.

First Responders. This includes police officers, firefighters, and emergency medical technicians. Two things make them tough audiences: the fact that they are jaded by life and the fact that they are already "over-trained." In reviewing the first point, it helps to know that the life philosophy of many of these folks is, "I've been there, done that. I've already seen it, heard it, or experienced it, so you can't teach me anything new." This is the case for even the newest rookie, who quickly develops the veteran's swagger, so as to best fit into the work and lifestyle culture that these difficult jobs create, in order to survive encounters in the field and with their peers.

In understanding the second point, while not every officer, firefighter, or EMT is necessarily college-educated or in possession of an advanced degree, they all have been through thousands of hours of classroom and field training. In other words, they've already sat through plenty of lectures, given by plenty of lecturers, long prior to your arrival in their lives.

In the best case, they will sit politely and not give the presenter too much of the usual "I'm too hip for the room" non-verbals, that is, eye rolling, heavy sighing, obvious sleeping. In the worst case, they will make lots of snappy comments from the back row and engage in all of the afore-listed non-verbals, plus a few new ones, like reading the newspaper, talking on their cell phones during the class, or leaving in the middle.

The keys to success with these tough people are simple: Already be one of them, either currently employed or retired from some police or fire agency. That's the key to credibility with them. They tend to listen best to people who are in their professions. However, if you're not part of their world, try these four strategies:

1. *Start with a little humility.* No long bios that emphasize what they may see as your "over-qualifications," that is, you're too smart to be standing in front of them. Begin with, "I'm not here to tell you how to do your jobs. I'm here to help you become even better at them."

2. *Connect with humor and visuals.* Use plenty of humor and stories; video clips; anecdotes related to crime, accidents, or safety; cartoons embedded into your PowerPoint™ presentations; and even slice-of-life, genuinely funny material that has nothing to do with your subject or their work.

3. *Protect their egos.* Never use individual, "do this in front of the whole group" exercises that can create ego problems if the person doing it fails. This population is hypersensitive to failure and prone to aggressive and even outrageous teasing of their peers, some of

which can last for years, as in, "Remember that time Dave dropped the CPR dummy off the table and the head rolled away. . . ." If you use exercises to teach certain concepts, have them work in ego-safe two- or three-person groups (dyads or triads, in our trade).

4. *Dress right for your role.* These groups often like to dress very casually while attending training programs (shorts, flip-flops, jeans, tank tops, and other casual wear). This doesn't mean you can do likewise. They do it because they wear uniforms all of the time and they like to "defy authority" by dressing somewhat sloppily. If the material you're covering is important and has an "executive," leadership, or management feel to it (new city policies, sexual harassment update), dress like an executive, leader, or manager. If the concepts are more hands-on (first-aid, safety procedures for new equipment), you can dress down more.

Judges and Attorneys. Like the previous group, this population is familiar with long hours of reading, research, and presenting their thoughts, strategies, and ideas to strangers. While they may recognize the need for continuing education as part of the way they demonstrate competence in the legal profession, they don't like it much. While they may be more polite than the first group, they can still act just as jaded toward new ideas.

And like the cops et al., the key to success with this group is to work or have worked in the legal field. Even a current or former paralegal, speaking to seasoned judges on a new issue, will have better success than a trainer who has no legal background.

Surviving with this group, who are similar to the police/fire/EMT folks, involves some differences:

1. This time, you should *provide a strong bio,* which highlights your educational achievements, writing, research, or work, teaching, or training experience. These people are used to being taught by true experts, not by trainers who are trying to fake their way through something they don't know or aren't comfortable with.

2. *Know in advance* why they are in front of you. Are they required to be there, or are they there because they have paid to come? Are you presenting at a conference where they will be getting Continuing Education Units (CEUs)?

3. *Be absolutely accurate* with your handouts, slides, and information. Any errors—significant or small—in your content can be a death sentence to the success of your training. They will either challenge you on it or leave the room. They are used to parsing the fine details in the English language, so the presence of typos, grammatical errors, or poorly constructed slides or handouts may cause them to question your credibility and the importance of your message. When in doubt, test your material with colleagues or, better yet, with another judge or attorney before you get in front of a group of them.

4. *Dress the part.* These people wear suits every day. Dress like one of them, even if it's a more casual environment where they are not wearing business attire. You can always remove a tie (men) or a jacket (ladies) if it feels comfortable to do so, but know that they are used to business-appropriate formalities in terms of appearances.

Medical Doctors and Nurses. The big problem here is time. This group usually doesn't feel like they have the time to give you, even if they are required to attend the training. If you're presenting to a cadre of medical doctors (who are just as or more "over-educated" as the previous two groups), you will probably see much multitasking going on. They will be reading other articles, writing notes about some other issues not related to yours, checking their pagers and cell phones every few minutes, leaving early, coming back late or not at all. You shouldn't take offense to this; it's just the nature of their business.

Paradoxically, nurses often like to attend training programs for the opposite reasons as their doctor counterparts: it gets them out of the clinic or off the hospital floor, and it gives them a justifiable break in their patient care duties. Whereas doctors are itching to get back to work, nurses look forward to the break in their work. Further, the training environment often gives them time to socialize with each other, catch up on hospital and personal gossip, and reconnect with colleagues they may rarely see because of the demands of their patients and their shift work.

Let's split the keys to success by profession, starting with the doctors:

1. Whatever program you've designed for them, go back and *cut the content and the time required in half.* "But wait!" you'll say, "I have some fascinating things to say, some valuable information to pass along." Great, now cut the time and the message in half. Whoever said, "Tell 'em what you're gonna tell 'em. Tell 'em. Then tell 'em what you just told 'em" was training doctors at that moment.

2. *Be positive your information is absolutely accurate.* Like judges and attorneys, doctors value precision. They place much importance on accurate information, especially cutting-edge information. They do not like to see or make errors in anything they do. While they may not challenge your data or concepts the way that judges or attorneys will, they will complain about it later. Wasting their time with inaccuracies is a cardinal sin in their world.

For nurses, the success keys are different:

1. *Make the learning process fun for them.* Unlike doctors, who will not risk their egos during training exercises, nurses are tactile, hands-on learners, and people-oriented folks. They like games or exercises that involve energy, activity, creativity, and especially talking. While medical doctors tend to want to exhibit an air of scientific detachment, nurses are into making connections, with themselves and with others. Their profession is different from most non-medical jobs because it is clouded with death and illness. They relish a break from the tedium and the negativity of their work. Give them group activities that allow them to laugh.

2. *Be liberal with breaks.* Give them enough time to reconnect with their colleagues and socialize a bit during the breaks. Play peaceful music via a soothing CD during this time and reinforce the need for them to take care of each other. Nursing is a high-burnout pro-

fession. The more you can do to make the training experience pleasant, the better you'll do on the feedback sheets.

3. *Allow them to vent, within reason.* While you don't want the training time to be lost to a gripe festival, it helps to let them have some time, as a group, to vent about what bothers them. Nursing is similar to being a doctor in its stress level (high human contact with patients in pain and in distress), without the benefits, pay, or prestige. You can simply write their complaints or concerns on a "Parking Lot" easel pad page and promise to deliver their words to management.

Non-English Speakers. Recognize that their presence in your session may not be their fault or even their choice. I once had to teach an eight-hour business writing class to an entire group of Filipina women who spoke almost no English and literally did not write one thing as part of their jobs. I protested before, during, and after my sessions that this training program was a waste of everyone's time, but the client was adamant that "everyone gets exposed to the same training, no matter their job." As such, these poor women looked at me like I was from Jupiter. They felt bad for me and I felt bad for them, so, after some very simple exercises, I just let them practice some skill-building, in both languages.

The keys to success (or just plain survival) with a group who does not speak much English are these:

1. If you have attendees with significant language barriers, you're doomed unless you can *get a translator* to help you teach the program. The best translators are not only native speakers of the language in question, but *simultaneous* translators as well. This means they have the skill and capacity to cover your words almost as fast as you can say them. Finding this kind of person is not a haphazard event; you need a professional. If you must train for groups who don't speak English sufficiently enough to get the basics of what you're saying, your client or your employer must provide a translator.

2. If you discover too late that the group has a language barrier, and if you don't have a translator (and can't reschedule to get one), you'll

likely need to *alter your original game plan* and improvise new learning approaches. Create table teams and put the person who speaks the best English in charge of each table. Give them simple and fun exercises that can help them help you meet your original training goals. If it's a new policy, ask the table "captains" to extract examples of the policy in action and how they plan to follow it in the future. If it's a skill-building training session, take the core behaviors or tasks you want them to learn and develop ways for the table captains to help their groups master them.

Blue-Collar Employees. There is no disparagement meant by this term; it's simply an identifier based on the type of work these folks tend to do, which is most often hourly (they're largely classified as non-exempt employees), sometimes outdoors, on an assembly line, in a factory, janitorial, maintenance or repair-related, manufacturing, or plain heavy, physical labor. And while I've met some poet laureates on the factory floor (for one example, you should read Ben Hamper's epic 1992 book, *Rivethead,* about his work as a riveter-cum-writer at the GM plant in Flint, Michigan), for the most part, these are people whose education level is more commonsense-based than textbook-based.

For several years, I taught a series of employee development seminars (stress management, most often) and policy update programs (sexual harassment, new-employee orientation, drug, alcohol, or workplace violence prohibitions, among others) to city and county employees, held usually at their respective city hall conference rooms, auditoriums, or city council/county supervisory chambers.

For nearly all of these programs, the orange-shirted public works employees (males and females) would be in heavy attendance. They would always sit in the back rows, but they would always serve as the best represented of all the employee populations.

Before I could pat myself on the back for my training skills, a colleague reminded me, "Of course they come to every training course the city or county offers. It gets them out of the hot sun, out of the rain, and out of the cabs of their work trucks for several hours. Your class, no matter what the subject is, serves as a mini-vacation for them." He was right, of course, and while they rarely caused problems, beyond a few sleeping with their sunglasses on, they never participated very much. I had to work much harder to draw them into the training conversations, exercises, and activities.

They aren't usually big on complexities in the training environment. Stick to exercises that are practical, fun, non-threatening to their egos, and somehow related to what they either do or need to learn. Like the first responders, in training situations where they fail or look less macho in front of their peers, they can be painfully cruel to each other, via teasing or ridicule. Make it easy for them to succeed. And since many of these employees have worked at their respective jobs for an amazingly long period—twenty-five to thirty-five years is not uncommon—make sure you draw them out and tap into their significant expertise when you can.

Ten Participants We Love to Hate

If the above list of tough audiences represents the macro picture—the forest, if you will—then let's look at the micro members—the individual trees—who can make tough topics even tougher. My key to defining a tough participant is fairly simple: Is this person's behavior or actions impacting the training program in a negative way? If the answer is yes, I feel I have to address it, either gently in a public format in front of the whole group, or more directly, when I pull the person off to the side at the first break.

While I'm using the concept of "hating" participants in a hyperbolic fashion, it's tough to feel much love when the following people populate your audience.

1. The Snorer

It would be humane and empathic of me to assume that perhaps this person had a rough night (up and down with an infant, a sick child, or a new puppy). However, it could also be the result of a hangover, or some passive-aggressive behavior, that is, "I don't really want to be here. So since they made me come, I'll just check out." While sleepers don't tend to bother others (besides me and my ego), Snorers do. Therefore, I make it a public point to ask someone sitting nearby to wake the person. Peer pressure usually keeps it from happening more than once.

2. The Challenger

This type of participant likes or wants to disagree with the presenter or other attendees on nearly every subject. In the best case, this person adds some spice and heat to the training session. In the worst case, this person manages to irritate everyone in the room by wasting time, injecting his or her rabid opinions into the most benign of issues (for example, "It is *not* too hot in here!").

If I see this starting early and having the potential to go on forever, I'll usually say to the person, "It's clear you feel strongly about the issue. We've heard your perspective. How about we hear from the others? If it's an issue to anyone else, we'll spend more time on it. If not, we have to move on."

I had a woman in one of my classes start her question with, "What I hear you *insinuating* is . . ." My mouth literally hung open, since I had made what I felt was a simple and innocuous statement, which she obviously took extreme offense to. I asked the group, "Did I *insinuate* my last remark?" A guy in the crowd shouted back, "No! You were fine. Let's move on!" So I did.

3. The Expert

Like the Challenger, this person not only intercedes constantly, to the distraction of the rest of the group, but he or she also corrects you and others as a way of showing his or her intelligence. This becomes tedious quickly and can polarize the crowd into two groups: Everyone Else versus or against the Expert.

When I haven't been on my toes and managed the group, I've allowed these people to poison the training process for others. In terms of full disclosure, these types of participants drive me crazy and tend to push my hot buttons faster than others. They sometimes start their comments with condescending lines like, "What you need to know about us is . . ." or "Let me fill you in on how things *really* work around here. . . ." In their haste to show others how smart they have made themselves, they interrupt the flow of the program, waste time that can't be recovered, and make people sigh or roll their eyes every time "the Expert" starts to speak.

Dealing with the Expert is tough, since you're always walking a fine line between silencing the person's ideas and preventing the person from ruining the training experience for others. In really extreme cases, I'll take the Expert aside after the first break and say, "Look, I can see you're a smart person. Can I ask you to hold your comments back enough to allow other people to speak? I'm not trying to kill your opinions; I just need to give the others more air time than they're getting now."

The gruesome truth is that if you speak to an Expert in this way, he or she will probably butcher you on the feedback sheets. If you don't bow to their intellects, you can predict they will hammer you on every part of your program. Some Experts believe you have nothing to contribute in this area and that, truth be told, *they* should be the ones teaching this class. Have the courage to speak to them privately, and take back control of *your* training program.

4. The Over-Eager Responder

This person can be harmless and irritating, or disruptive and irritating. Over-Eagers know the answer to *every* question you ever ask. They will shoot their hands skyward or shout out the answer before the question even gets all the way out of your mouth. This is great if you're trying to win a game show and not so great during a training program. By hogging the intellectual spotlight, they can make other people feel discouraged that they either don't know as much or don't get a chance to prove how much they know to the presenter and the group.

Over-Eagers seem to want to overcompensate for low self-esteem issues by reminding others they are smart, capable, and worthy. Like Challengers and Experts, they can become room dividers. The best ways to deal with them are to simply call on other people for their answers, remind them that they've already contributed quite a bit and it's good to hear from others, or to take them aside at the break and have the same discussion as you would have with the Expert, about sharing the air time.

5. The Hostility Poster Child

It's clear from this person's over-the-top behavior that he or she really doesn't want to be there. This attendee comes back from breaks or lunches late, gives you lots of audible sighs or yawns, and makes a big production out of packing up and leaving early. One audience member is bad enough, but more than one (a mini-mutiny, if you will) can be quite disruptive. This approach—"I'm just too hip for the room"—distracts other people who actually did come to learn.

I have one usual response in my tool kit for this person, which involves using the behavioral concept of *extinction.* This approach says that if you ignore certain behaviors and give no signs that they affect you, you can sometimes extinguish the behavior. Hostile types seem to believe that even negative attention is good attention. When he or she does a hostile act—snorting "Huh!" at something I've said that he or she disagrees with—I simply stop, smile directly at the offender, and let a few moments of silence pass. Since silence builds tension, I wait until it's palpable to the group that I've heard the behavior, then I get back to work. Their behavior is not often lost on the entire group. Sometimes peer pressure—as when they realize they're suddenly caught and on the spot—can keep their antics down to a minimum.

6. The Wrong Course/Wrong Participant

This is the attendee who is clearly in over his or her head. Like the confused passenger who gets on the wrong airplane, this person is in the wrong place at the wrong time. I've seen frontline employees who either signed up for or were assigned to attend a management-level program. That's great, except they don't supervise anyone. I've seen others come to a negotiating program just to learn how to get a better deal on a car the next time they have to buy one. Then there are employees who come to sales training courses when they don't sell anything, ever, to anyone.

Sometimes it's hard to tell whose fault it is for this bad fit of wrong employee/wrong content. Sometimes the employee's supervisor is the culprit, other times the employee misreads the description of the program, or reads it correctly and signs up anyway. The hardest part of this issue is that you don't usually find out until you're already rolling. It's during the table-team introductions or when we're going around the room with individual introductions that I get the fish-out-of-water news. So do you embarrass these people by asking them to leave? Or do you welcome them and invite them to participate as they see fit? I usually choose the latter, simply because I want to protect all the attendees from undue stress, and because I rationalize it away by believing the person may get something useful out of the program that could benefit his or her career later on.

7. The Passive-Mute Statue

For whatever reason, these types of people arrive at the training room, take their seats, and then proceed to stare at you for the duration of the program. They don't ask questions; they don't chat much with their co-workers, colleagues, or other participants; and they don't respond to you unless you ask them pointedly. They're usually polite, non-confrontational, and exceedingly quiet. There are several issues at work here: (1) they're often quite smart but they may have language issues, so they're embarrassed to show their communication limitations; (2) they're in the wrong course and don't want to admit it, so they'll sit through the whole session, full of pride, not willing to get up and leave; or (3) they're angry at whoever made them go to the course, so they pay it back with passive behavior.

As a trainer, I'm aware that I have to engage with all the other people in the room too. Because the Passives are low-maintenance (they don't argue, challenge, or disrupt), it's easy to ignore them. When I'm faced with this type of participant, I make several attempts to draw them out, often to no avail. So as time and the course roll along, I rationalize passing over them by saying, "Well, if they really *wanted* to participate, they would participate, right? I can't make them talk. I can't make them go out of their comfort zone, can I?"

Some of my training colleagues refuse to take no for an answer from these folks, and will go the extra mile to draw them out, using their names frequently, and calling on them to lead certain exercises or discussions. I usually stop if my third attempt is met with more passivity. The best you can do is to try and keep them connected to the subject and to the rest of the group.

One last irony of the Passive type is found on the feedback sheets. They will either love the course and love you, and you won't know that they were pleased with the program until you read their glowing comments, or they will hate the program and hate you, writing comments like, "Instructor didn't engage with me. Instructor failed to connect with group. Instructor seemed 'unavailable.'" The rub is that these comments seem to appear most frequently when I've gone way out of my usual way to ask them to participate.

8. The Jokester

A little of this guy (and it's rarely a female culprit here) goes a really long way. His smart-mouth comments, snide remarks, and (my favorite) his witty asides, loudly stage-whispered to his pals, don't do much to endear him to the trainer or the other participants. There is more than a little passive-aggressiveness going on here, aimed at you, the organization, the bosses, and/or others. Some of this guy's behavior is purely attention-getting, other parts are related to low self-esteem, and some of it is simply hateful and hurtful.

My strategy for these guys is twofold: Let them run on for a bit and wait for their lame jokes to fall flat in the public arena and/or pull them aside and give them the same speech I give to the Expert, the Challenger, or the Over-Eager.

9. The Dumb Guy

Sometimes it's quite hard to tell whether this participant is pulling your leg or really lacks the tools to cope in the modern world. During a training session for assembly-line employees at a manufacturing plant, I had an attendee ask me this question (loudly and in front of the whole group) while he was trying to fill out a form: "What's the date today?"

I said, "The seventeenth."

He said, "No, what's the date."

I said, "April 17th."

Now suddenly angry, he stood up and said, "I'm asking you again, what is the date today? Monday? Tuesday? Are you gonna tell me or what?"

Was this intentional, simply a unique way to get under my skin (which succeeded), or was he really not sure of the day of the week? I'm still puzzled over the exchange, which seemed to bother him just as much as it bothered me. I kept a wary eye on him for the remainder of the session and he left red-faced and still angry. The HR director, who had witnessed this as well, said, "Well,

I guess that shows why he's still a temp [temporary worker] and not full-time with us."

10. The Poster Child for Political Correctness

H. L. Mencken once said, "A Puritan is someone who is desperately afraid that, somewhere, someone might be having a good time."

The Politically Correct (PC) attendee is hypersensitive to the trainer making any untoward references to gender, age, sex, race, politics, animal rights, the environment, or religion during the training program. They like their seminars in one flavor—plain vanilla. PCs see themselves as highly in touch with the culture of their times. They become filled with righteous indignation whenever someone else's beliefs or approach differs from theirs. Here's a typical exchange after the PC has struck:

HR Director: "Someone complained about that example you used about polar bears in your training program."

Trainer: "Oh? Who was that? What did he or she say?"

HR Director: "She took offense to your reference."

Trainer: "Did you hear what I said about polar bears?"

HR Director: "No, I wasn't there. But for the future, we don't want to upset anyone, so don't make that reference again."

Here the PC person has corrupted your client, who didn't experience what was said or hear it in the right context. Yet some clients are afraid to upset this person by simply saying, "Okay. I hear you. I'll look into it," *and then not bothering the trainer by bringing it up if it's not truly offensive or significant.*

To hear my father, Karl, tell it, the problem with PCs is that, somewhere along the way, they have lost their sense of humor. They tend to want to see the world as one big global village, when in reality, it is and always will be, filled with lots of people who are vastly different from each other. You should certainly *always* monitor your training materials, handouts, slides, exercises, and approaches for obvious signs of overt or covert racism, ageism, or gender bias. However, you don't always have to apologize for harmless remarks made in the context of the moment.

When I'm confronted by these PC people (my track record is about one hostile encounter per year), I listen carefully and say, "You could be right. I'll consider how I discuss the issue for the next time." This doesn't mean I necessarily agree, just that I've heard the issue and I'll evaluate my response in the future.

11. Bonus Participant (Scary, Odd, or Just Curious)

Here's a novel one: You're teaching a course in a public facility, such as a hotel ballroom, a conference room in a library, a city hall, or a community center. Right in the middle of your gig, in walks a transient, filthy of beard and reeking of unmetabolized ethanol. He politely asks the group if they have any spare change or an extra cigarette or two.

Or, how about the locally well-known mentally ill woman, with hair like Medusa and a personality to match, who strolls in while you're speaking, sits down at one of the back tables, and starts thumbing through the handouts?

How about the older, retired gent, with plenty of time on his hands, who approaches the glass back window outside the training room, cups his hands around his eyes, and stares in at you for 45 minutes or so? Each of these Bonus Members can create anxiety or confusion for both the trainer and the participants. Be prepared for the unusual "guest," politely ask the fun-seeker to leave, and when the group has calmed itself (some participants tend to have valid security concerns when strangers walk in), get right back to work, as if it hasn't bothered you.

Nothing Lasts Forever

One of my training colleagues, Jeanne McGuire from the Fallbrook, California–based firm, McGuire-Pratson Consultants, has a knack for picking me up whenever I'm feeling down about a program or a group. Whenever she and I team-teach and we're facing an apathetic or unruly group, she leans over to me and whispers, "The good news is that it's almost over. We're almost done here."

What's funny about this remark is that she usually says it about 3 minutes into the start of the program! We use it as a running gag all day and carry it over into breakfast at the hotel coffee shop the next morning.

In many instances, the client knows it's a tough crowd; *that's why they brought you in, so they don't have to do it themselves.*

Not everybody hates the program or you, and if some do, then always remember that it's more about what you represent (the need for them to attend or to make performance or behavioral changes) than an attack on you personally.

In the training life, sometimes you eat the dog and sometimes the dog eats you. I've taught the exact same four-hour program to two groups in one day and the differences between the first and the second was like the difference between a fish and a bicycle. If the first group made you miserable, eat your lunch, catch your breath, and go after the second group with as much enthusiasm as you have when it's all going great.

There's always another program on another day, where chances are better that they will love you (or at least like or even tolerate you) again.

4

Employee Orientation Programs

Walk groundly, talk profoundly, drink roundly, sleep soundly.

—William Hazlitt (1778–1830)

Key

Depending on the size of the organization, the orientation process for new employees can range from casual to intense, from an hour-long chat and a quick tour of the facility ("Here's your cubicle, there's the bathroom, and the cafeteria is down the hall") to up to two or even three days of in-class lectures, material reviews, policy manual discussions, and the like. Know that this is an anxious time for new employees. The orientation process either creates a success model for them to follow or it leaves them feeling alienated.

Studies tell us that an effective orientation program plays a significant role in employee retention. Always keep in mind that, outside of their HR department contacts, you may be the first "real" representative of the company that these employees see. Your initial welcome, a solid program (that answers their questions, allays their fears, and gives them a chance to meet one another), and a strong wrap-up can give them a sense of inclusion and confidence that will get them all started on the right feet.

Usual Audience

This session is for new employees at every level, save for perhaps the C-level, who tend not to attend orientations with the rank and file. It's useful and usual in some organizations for a senior member of the organization to spend a few moments welcoming the new hires. A few kind words from a chief executive or similar high-powered manager can send an important signal that the company cares enough to provide orientation and that it's a valuable way to learn the ins and outs of the organizational climate and culture.

Members of the HR department should sit through the sessions, ready to answer questions about the Policy and Procedures Manual, cafeteria-style benefits packages (medical, dental, vision, etc.), and other questions related to pay periods, direct deposit, and so on. Whether you're an internal trainer, familiar with the firm, or an external trainer, brought in to provide your personal touch or expertise to the orientation program, you should welcome the presence of HR people to fill in the knowledge gaps for you and the participants.

Best Length

This depends on the size of the organization, the amount of material to be covered, and who will "guest speak" along with the trainer. Some programs feature an appearance from various department heads, typically from HR, Security/Safety, Benefits, Payroll, Facilities, Customer Service, and others. This is not a requirement, but it does add some flavor to the sessions and helps new people put names to faces and vice versa. It also gives the department heads a chance to speak about what is important to them, brag a bit about their existing teams, and talk about how the various departments fit together and serve each other, directly and indirectly.

The more people involved as speakers, the more time you'll need. Plan for a minimum of four to eight hours. It's usually best to complete the orientation process in one day, since time is now money once these folks are on the payroll. Some organizations provide extended orientation programs, going up to two or even three days, but most management teams believe one-day sessions are sufficient. The reasoning here is that most employees will get on-the-job and department-specific instruction when they get to their new position.

Basic Training Themes

For some employees who are new to the job world, attending a formal orientation program is like getting a drink from a fire hose. They can feel overwhelmed after the first 30 minutes, so try not to overload the participants with too much, too soon.

Start with a warm and sincere introduction. Thank the new hires for being part of the organization and promise them that, although you'll provide a lot of information in a short period of time, you will always make time for their questions and answers.

Here's why we conduct new-hire orientation programs:

- To provide a positive view of the organization, by being inclusive and welcoming of them.
- To let them know what will be expected from them.
- To help them understand our boundaries, their responsibilities, and our rules.
- To have us teach them the "real rules," and not learn them from their co-workers.
- To help with their retention and to help them complete their probationary periods successfully.
- To help them absorb the company culture and assimilate quickly.
- To build their morale at an early stage.
- To give them access to the people and the resources to help them succeed, that is, HR, Payroll, Information Services, Technical Support, and others.
- To give them a chance to succeed, on equal ground, with their co-workers.

- To build a sense of connection, cohesion, and stability, so they can be productive sooner.

- To give us a chance to see each new employee in our environment. (How do or will they interact with us and each other? Will we get any early signs of future star performers or potential slackers?)

Current Organizational Policies

This is usually the moment where all employees are introduced to the Policies and Procedures Manual for the organization. Depending on the size and sophistication of the HR department, this manual can be a bit (too) brief or (overly) lengthy. Like "Goldilocks and the Three Bears," neither is just right. A P&P manual that is not very complete will allow for legal or procedural loopholes and can lead to controversies later when it comes to managing employee behavior, productivity, or performance issues. A P&P manual that is too weighty simply never gets read. More organizations are moving toward a twofold approach: they put the entire P&P manual on the company intranet and also provide a more readable paper version to the employees during orientation.

The main issue with the size and scope of the P&P manual is that we're trying to strike the right balance for every employee between, "It's not covered in my manual" and "I never read that, so therefore, I'm not bound by it or responsible for it." I have seen employment litigation cases where the employee's defense was, "No one ever told me I couldn't do it," even though the behavior was expressly prohibited in the P&P manual. "This set of documents," the company argues, "was given to you at orientation." The follow-up defense to *that* statement is often, "*Lots* of confusing documents were given to me at orientation. I couldn't possibly have read all of them."

If the organization has provided a physical policy manual, then initiating a few look-up exercises with the new-hires (as in, "Please find our policy on sexual harassment, so we can discuss it. . . .") can help to familiarize them with the manual.

As such, good orientation programs provide consistent reminders that "You can find full and complete descriptions of these policies and procedures on our intranet site or in this full version of the P&P manual, which you have just been given. Please speak to your supervisor or call HR if you have questions or concerns about the language of any of our policies. You are fully responsible for following them, even if we don't cover them today."

The Organizational Culture and Climate

In the January 2003 issue of *HR Magazine,* Salt Lake City employment law attorney Jathan W. Janove writes succinctly about what he calls the employer's need to "speak softly and carry a big stick." Using the Teddy Roosevelt adage as a model for better employee relations and the need for effective orientation, he puts it this way:

> In the employer-employee context, "speaking softly" means expressing management's expectations of employees in a manner that respects their dignity and keeps the supervisor's own ego in check. The "big stick" symbolizes the supervisor's commitment to results. Both elements are necessary. Without the speech, employees will lack direction. Without the big stick, employees will not understand the necessity of obtaining the desired results and will confuse soft speech with a soft will. All too often, employees are left to their own devices in carving out a path to success or failure with their new employers. They receive a general orientation on company policy, procedure, and practices. As for crucial performance and behavioral expectations that will determine their future, however, management is largely silent—at least until problems arise. Conversely, some companies induct new hires into a form of boot camp in which employees are drilled on the rules and warned of dire potential consequences should they fail to do the do's or succeed in doing the don'ts. Both approaches create unnecessary problems and lost opportunities. In the first approach, where there is neither "voice" nor "stick," some new hires will nevertheless manage to stumble forward

toward success and figure out the path on their own. However, many employees will miss out on success, not because they lacked ability, but because they needed clearer directions as to the desired path and the importance of taking it. In the second approach, where the voice booms, the tendency for new hires will be to keep their heads down— go along, get along, and don't stick your neck out. This approach will cost employers that discretionary energy that employees offer if they are properly motivated. It's this energy that leads employees to take risks on behalf of the company, to show initiative and to volunteer ideas that help the employer exploit valuable opportunities or avoid costly mistakes.* [pp. 73–74]

Which approach to orientation the organization you're training for has taken will have a lot to say about the success of your efforts. There is only one chance at success with this program; without a follow-up process or a "buddy system" where new employees are teamed with new employees, they may only come before you this one time.

The (Real) Purpose of the Program

There are usually three reasons why an employee is terminated from his or her position: (1) attendance failures/problems (late, not there, leaves early); (2) violation of policies and procedures (you can't smoke in the dynamite factory); or (3) work performance. The first is the easiest to document and the last is the hardest, so, not surprisingly, upwards of 75 percent of people who are fired from their jobs are fired for attendance reasons.

Therefore, a thorough, effective, and inviting employee orientation program should not only address these issues, but by doing so we can help to avoid them or lessen their impact, for both the employee and the organization, down the road.

---

*Reprinted with permission of *HR Magazine,* published by the Society for Human Resource Management, Alexandria, VA.

Their Learning Keys

As a reminder, "Learning Keys" are those critical points you (and the client or your organization) want the attendees to come away with after the training session.

For the subject of orientation, this includes the company mission statement, organizational charts, HR procedures, pay and benefits, safety and security issues, copies of the Policy and Procedures Manual, how new employees can use and access their e-mail accounts and computer networks, the Employee Assistance Program contact information, and the company-sponsored benefits available to all.

Your Teaching Keys

At the start of the training program, here is what most new hires are concerned about:

- Will this be a boring class or will I really get something from it, besides just mounds of paper and rule books?

- Are they going to give me too much information, too soon?

- What are their expectations of me?

- Will I have to fill out a lot of forms?

- How long will this take?

- What about my pay and benefits?

- Who is my boss?

- Who *really* runs things around here?

At the end of the training session, here's what the new employee will want to have proven to him or her: "Tell me that this is a safe, stable place to work. Tell me that I made the right choice by coming to work here. Help me fit in right away, by knowing what everyone else already knows about this place—the people, the work that is done here, our products or services, and our customers."

Your Success Tools

PowerPoint™ slides and plenty of support from HR; copies of the P&P Manual; name plates and badges for the new hires.

Potholes and Sandpits

As attorney Janove suggested, now is not the time to scare, intimidate, or overload new employees with threats from the HR or "Corporate Rule Book." This should be a time of both welcoming and boundary setting, of speaking of hope for their future successes and providing them with the same rules of accountability, responsibility, and performance as the current employees.

If you use some form of a collaborative program, as the Necessary Nine PowerPoint™ slides at the end of the chapter suggest, then you'll need to be an effective ringmaster to get the various department heads or spokespeople up and through their respective material. Meet each speaker prior to the session and say, "I'll be keeping time for us all, so look for me as I stand in the back of the room. If I point to my watch, that means you have about 5 minutes to wrap up your session. Thanks in advance for helping to keep us all on time."

Some Fine Points

If there was ever a time to add some enthusiasm and pizzazz to your training presentation, this is probably the best example. What you're doing with new employees is more about "selling" than training. This is the lone opportunity to create a positive and lasting first impression about the organization. Anything you can do to help them enjoy this experience, allay their fears, and start them off right will be appreciated by the department heads and supervisors across the organization.

One of the only positives to come from the 9/11 tragedies is that it helped reorient American businesses to the need for better safety and security policies, new procedures, and updated training. The orientation process provides a useful opportunity to tell employees that we are now living and working in what is being called the "new normal." As such, we will pay more attention to issues that in the past were glossed over in the orientation process, including evacuation plans; mandatory wearing of ID badges; access control concerns; visitor and vendor access policies; first-aid equipment; CPR training; fire drills; bomb or phone threat responses; and domestic and workplace violence prevention awareness and responses.

SAMPLE TRAINING PROGRAM SLIDES: THE NECESSARY NINE

Use the following slides to craft the core of your program, adding or deleting as you see fit. The design will depend on the audience, length, current policies, the culture of the organization, and the (real) purpose of the program.

COMPANY ORIENTATION AGENDA

Welcome and Introductions

Our Mission Statement

HR Orientation

Payroll and Benefits Orientation

Health, Safety, and Security Orientation

Computer Network Orientation

Our Policies and Procedures Manual

Perks and Benefits

Welcome and Introductions

Greeting and welcome by HR Department representative

Greeting and welcome by Senior Executive

Greeting and welcome by Trainer/Facilitator

Introductions of new employees: name, job, prior work history or background, hobbies or interests away from work

Our Mission Statement

Our Organizational Chart—divisions, locations, products, and services

Our Chief Executives—CEO, CFO, CIO, and others

Our VPs or Division Heads

Our Department Heads

Examples of Departmental Mission Statements

Our Goals, Our Customers

HR Orientation

Welcome and introductions of HR staff

Hours of work, attendance, lunch and break policies

Vacation, sick leave, and holiday policies

Probation periods, promotion, and job transfer opportunities

Brief overview of Policies and Procedures Manual

Behavior Requirements—overview of sexual harassment, hostile work environment, drug and alcohol, workplace violence, respect for diversity, and EEO policies

Employee Assistance Program information and contact numbers

Facility tour, if necessary, to cover: parking, restrooms, cafeteria, first-aid stations, evacuation procedures, safety or security procedures

Payroll and Benefits Orientation

Welcome by Payroll and Benefits Coordinator

Paydays, time cards, hourly sheets, overtime, and salary policies

Cafeteria-Style Benefits Plans: medical, dental, vision, long-term care, catastrophic care, life insurance, family member coverage, and others

Retirement plans, 401(k) information

Additional Benefits: education and tuition reimbursement, retirement matching, stock options, and others

Health, Safety, and Security Orientation

Welcome by Safety/Security/Risk Management Staff

Safety and Security Plan: ID badges, end-of-the-day security procedures, information protection, visitor and vendor policies

First-Aid, Medical, Fire, and Other Emergencies

Evacuation Plans and Meeting Locations

Drug and Alcohol Prohibitions

Workplace Violence Prevention Plan

Computer Network Orientation

Welcome by Information Services representative

Brief overview of network design, equipment, location

Employee PC usage policies, prohibitions

Security and password policies, back-up policies, emergency help

E-mail accounts

Intranet use

Our Policies and Procedures Manual

Overview of critical areas by HR staff

Specific discussions on behavioral issues

Intranet P&P sites

Question-and-answer period

Sign and return P&P manual/orientation
sheet for employee's file

Perks and Benefits

Floating Holidays, "Mental Health Days," Discretionary Days, Flex-Time or Tele-Commuting Options

Company "Store": employee discounts on company products or services

Recognition and Rewards Programs: attendance, retirement, cost-savings ideas, celebrating team successes

Quality of Work Life Support: credit union, fitness center, cafeteria, company sports teams, community sponsorships and charities

5

Sexual Harassment Programs for Employees and Supervisors

It is human nature to think wisely and act foolishly.

—Anatole France

Key

Even in our supposedly enlightened business times, the subject of sexual harassment continues to garner more litigation threats and actual civil suits than any other workplace behavior-related issue. It's not a luxury item for the training budget dollars; it's an absolute yearly requirement.

Usual Audience

Is the group all supervisors (my first preference), all frontline employees, or a mixture (my least favorite combination)? My preference is to train to the people you have, at their level. If you have managers and supervisors only, teach them what they need to do to stay current and legal by asking a critical question: Will you, as the supervisor, have to *investigate* a claim of sexual harassment or simply *report* it to Human Resources? The difference is critical, since if the answer is yes to the former, you'll have to teach an investiga-tive/interviewing module as well.

If the group is frontline employees only, let them vent a bit about the issue when you first start, but quickly take control of the room by being authori-tative (in a pleasant and assertive way). I believe the secret to success with this subject starts with defining the boundaries (ranging from understanding the misuse of physical closeness in social situations, a "no-touching" orientation, no risqué jokes, and so on), giving people the limits of those boundaries, and explaining both the consequences to sexual harassers and the protections pro-vided to victim-employees.

Best Length

While you probably don't need eight hours, an hour is not enough. My pref-erence is to spend at least two hours with the employees and two to four hours with the supervisors. (As an example of a government-mandated length, in 2005, the California legislature passed Assembly Bill 1825, which requires all employers with fifty or more employees to provide at least two hours of biannual supervisory training on this subject.) With breaks, questions, and a lively group, you'll need every minute.

Basic Training Themes

As a subject, most participants view sexual harassment training right up with having their roofs re-tarred or going to the dentist, that is, necessary but not very much fun. More accurately, frontline employees (mostly the male ones) who come to these training sessions have several vague yet irritating thoughts roaming through their heads: "Why am I here? I've been good. I've not said or done anything that could be sexually harassing. Or have I? Geez, there was that time last month over by the copy machine where I said, 'Hey Mary! Did you hear the one about the rabbi and the cowboy playing golf?' Uh-oh. . . ."

Not surprisingly, the line supervisors who must attend this training have similar conversations in their heads: "Why am I here? Are we having some sort of sweeping epidemic of this behavior? What am *I* supposed to do about this problem? Do I have to monitor every single conversation in my work area? Can I be sued? Isn't this whole program just a reaction to a bunch of politically correct reactionaries?"

As a result of these intrusive thoughts, most of the participants are in a jolly mood once the trainer takes the stage.

Current Organizational Policies

Does a sexual harassment policy already exist? When was the last time it was revised? Have all employees been trained on this policy yet, or is that one of the purposes of the training?

In this modern era, just about every viable business organization has a sexual harassment policy, which is supposed to define appropriate workplace behaviors, prohibitions, sanctions for perpetrators, and support for victims.

If the employees routinely deal with taxpayers, customers, and/or vendors, then it's important that the organizational policy addresses cases of *third-party harassment* as well. It should be made clear in the policy that the company will investigate and attempt to stop all cases of sexual harassment or a hostile work environment, even if the prohibited conduct involves non-employees. In other words, if the guy who fixes the copier sexually harasses one of our people, we will intervene.

The Organizational Culture and Climate

In some organizations, the culture for sexual harassment training sometimes starts with the idea that "we shouldn't irritate any of the important people by making them attend." This group could include the senior scientists, technical people, VP-level sales staff, and others. If the line employees must attend the program and managers are noticeably absent from most sessions, believe you me, you'll see it in the feedback sheets. When it comes to the tough topic of sexual harassment, the message that senior management should send to every employee, at every level, is clear: "This is important. Because it is important, the training is mandatory."

The (Real) Purpose of the Program

It helps if you can divine this from senior management. Is one possible reason for this training program a response to a surge in the problem? In other words, is this training day event-driven? Is another reason that it's an annual compliance session? Is it part of a recent hiring expansion and part of new-employee orientation? Or is it simply time to provide a refresher on the issue, since much time has passed since the last training program?

Their Learning Keys

Company policies, definitions, reporting procedures, the supervisor's responsibilities, sanctions for violators of the policy, protections for the victims, the legal ramifications (personal liability is now possible for all employees, not just supervisors), access to the company Employee Assistance Program (if applicable).

Your Teaching Keys

Focus on the positive, not the legal. Use humor appropriately and carefully. Don't embarrass any person or group to make a point. This subject can create tension in the room, which can be compounded into a verbal minefield for both the trainer and the participants. You must stay on track, on point, and on slide. You must avoid and/or control the need some participants have to sabotage the program through too many sidebar discussions and off-the-wall questions. These are usually designed to confuse you and the rest of the group, thereby muddying the waters so no one gets any benefit during the session.

Your Success Tools

Strong PowerPoint™ slides; participant materials (which have been pre-approved by HR and/or the company attorney); an appropriate video; a training design based on understanding of the current written organizational policy, which should entail recognizing warning signs, supporting victims, stopping the behaviors, and getting back to business without creating excess controversy.

Potholes and Sandpits

Saying or allowing the wrong kinds of jokes, beating people over the head with the "Law Book," allowing the discussion to get out of hand, and taking sides are all recipes for a training-day disaster. However, the biggest ingredient in the screw-it-up stewpot can be a dollar sign.

Follow the logic here: Let's say you've been a diligent researcher on the Internet and have come up with scores of sexual-harassment-based lawsuits, where the victimized plaintiff has been vindicated and healed, and the organization has been corrected, via a major cash award to the injured party.

Be aware that you're now handling dynamite. Imagine that a certain employee, sitting in the training room with a group of co-workers, sees himself or herself as cunning, aggrieved, and perfectly capable of manipulating "the system."

This person hears you rattle off a list of plaintiff awards: "A woman in Illinois received $3.4 million when she sued her firm . . ." or "A man in Michigan settled his case with his former employer for $2.7 million. . . ."

So perhaps now the seed has been planted, in the manipulating employee's mind, for future litigation. You can hear this person's thought process now: "Easy Street here I come! I can sue and get some 'go away' money from these idiots who have mistreated me for so long. Let me take some notes as the trainer talks about more and more 'hostile work environment' claims. . . ."

Stay away from any mention of specific cases, with either employee or supervisor groups. The employees may have a person licking his or her chops in anticipation of a lottery-esque settlement, and the supervisors will immediately fear their houses will be taken away after they're named in some sort of civil action.

If either group asks, say this:

"We've certainly seen an increase in the number of EEO-related investigations in this area. Some have turned into lawsuits; most are settled without a civil suit. As long as you're following the guidelines of our formal, written sexual harassment policy, and acting within the scope of your employment, as an employee or a supervisor, it's nearly impossible to be sued successfully. As long as you're doing your work the way you've been told, or managing your people as you've been trained, your organization will support you. It's when people go outside of company policies that they put themselves at risk. This issue is one of the primary reasons I'm here today: to teach you this material and review our policy in careful detail."

Some Fine Points

Allow participants to vent, but within reason. Have a representative from HR introduce the program, saying, "We're doing this training today because it's important, not because this is a rampant problem at this facility." (Omit the last statement if it *is* a rampant problem, of course.)

It's perfectly acceptable to mention the inherent tension in the room that this subject can create. For many behavior-based training subjects, I frequently start with, "How many of you were so excited about this topic that you couldn't *wait* to get here?" or "This is one of those tough training topics that's hard to talk about at this hour of the morning (or right after lunch). . . ."

SAMPLE LEADER'S GUIDE/ TRAINING MODULE OUTLINE

Use what you need from the following topic outline to design your own program.

MODULE 1: INTRODUCTION TO SEXUAL HARASSMENT PREVENTION

As a workplace subject, sexual harassment is certainly not "new news." The subject has been around as long as people have worked together. As a training issue, sexual harassment is one of the most significant and important topics you'll encounter as an employee. Along with workers' compensation cases and injuries or deaths due to safety problems, sexual harassment is probably the one topic most connected to lawsuits, litigation, and multi-million-dollar jury awards.

As such, it's critically important to understand what employees, at every level in the organization, should and should not do, when interacting with each other, customers, vendors, or other non-employees.

Since the implementation of Title VII of the Civil Rights Act (and subsequent court rulings in 1972 and 1986), this subject has become a training staple in every intelligent organization. You need to know how sexual harassment is defined, what constitutes sexual harassment, and what you can do to avoid violating your policy or getting disciplined, terminated, or sued.

The bottom line is that sexual harassment is about treating everyone fairly, decently, and with the maturity that is necessary to understand and comply with the workplace rules surrounding this complex issue.

- The law (and our behavioral-based policies) entitles every employee, at every level, to a "harassment-free" work environment.
- You have a duty to know your company's policies and procedures regarding sexual harassment.
- As an employee or a supervisor, you can be individually liable for sexual harassment. This means you can be disciplined, terminated, or even sued as a result of this conduct.
- Sexual harassment is considered *outside* the course and scope of your employment, meaning we do not allow it, under any circumstances, as part of your job or work duties.

MODULE 2:
"QUID PRO QUO" SEXUAL HARASSMENT

Sexual harassment can be generally defined as

Unwelcome sexual advances, requests for sexual favors, and other verbal or physical conduct of a sexual nature.

The Equal Employment Opportunity Commission (EEOC) defines sexual harassment in two distinct ways: what is commonly called "quid pro quo" (a Latin phrase meaning "this for that") and/or allowing or creating a sexually harassing or sexually hostile work environment.

Quid pro quo sexual harassment consists of receiving job benefits based on sexual favors. Examples include a supervisor forcing his or her employee to provide sexual favors in order to obtain or keep a job, get a promotion, a pay raise, preferred work shift, easier work duties, and so forth.

People often compare this type of sexual harassment to the old Hollywood "casting couch" scenario, where actors and actresses could only get work if they had sex with a casting director.

It typically involves some implicit or explicit term or condition of employment, typically between someone who holds a position of power over an employee.

The gender of either party makes no difference. It can involve a female supervisor and a male employee, or even a boss and employee of the same sex.

MODULE 3: "HOSTILE ENVIRONMENT" SEXUAL HARASSMENT

This type is defined as *"unwanted, unwelcome, and repetitive visual, verbal, or physical conduct based on sex or of a sexual nature that unreasonably interferes with an employee's work performance or creates an intimidating, hostile, or offensive work atmosphere."*

The key to understanding this type of sexual harassment starts with your awareness of the phrase "unwelcome, unwanted, and repetitive."

Not every encounter between employees is sexual harassment. A sexually hostile environment is generally thought, by a reasonable person, to be caused by an unwelcome activity, an unwanted activity, and a repetitive activity (meaning that it happens regularly and/or even after the person has been told to stop).

We can define a hostile environment in general terms, as typically involving sexually oriented

- Jokes, posters, photos, or comments

- E-mails, letters, phone calls, messages of a sexual nature

- Touching, hugging, rubbing, or blocking the way of an employee

- Looks (leering or ogling) and non-verbal gestures

- Favoritism toward an employee based on his or her gender, style of provocative dress, or flirting behavior

- Sharing inappropriate personal sexual information with another employee, for example, "weekend tales"

MODULE 4:
SEXUAL HARASSMENT—
PEOPLE AND PLACES

It's becoming more difficult to define "the workplace." Recent court cases have created a very wide definition of where we do our work. The building where we work is certainly one "workplace," but depending on the circumstances and the context of an employee's behavior, the workplace can also be defined as

- Business trips to conferences, seminars, or meetings

- The car or truck you use as part of your work

- Lunches or other meals

- "Official" company-sanctioned parties or gatherings

- Anywhere you function as an employee of the company

This means that all employees must consider their "at-work" conduct to include these non-traditional work locations. Sexual harassment prevention is about respect for other employees' boundaries. It can occur over a lunchtime meal, just as it could in an office.

WHO CAN SEXUALLY HARASS YOU?

Sexual harassment is not as much about gender as it is about power, control, or the desire for one or more people to make an employee feel shamed or embarrassed about his or her sexuality. The usual scenario involving a male boss sexually harassing his female secretary has grown to include female supervisors harassing male employees; co-workers at all levels harassing each other; a group of female employees sexually harassing their male boss; males sexually harassing other males; or gay employees harassing or being harassed by other gay or straight employees.

Further, the nature of the employment relationship is not as significant as the *conduct* of the person doing the harassing. Third parties can be just as guilty of sexual harassment as a co-worker. As such, depending on the services your business provides, you could be sexually harassed by a customer, taxpayer, patient, parent, vendor, consultant, volunteer, or part-time or temporary employee.

You have the right to report *any* sexually harassing behavior to your supervisor and/or to Human Resources, even if the person harassing you is not an employee of the company.

MODULE 5:
THE SUPERVISOR'S GUIDE TO
SEXUAL HARASSMENT INVESTIGATIONS

- Respond immediately. (Take the complaint and take it seriously.)

- Determine the type of sexual harassment (quid pro quo and/or hostile work environment?).

- Consult with Human Resources as soon as possible.

- Decide whether there is a policy violation. (Not every issue is sexual harassment; some are related to general harassment based on the employee's race, religion, gender, etc.)

- Identify the participants. (If possible, review their personnel files and your own notes from previous incidents, if any.)

- If required by HR or your company policy, interview all participants, including the victim(s), any witness(es), and the harasser(s).

- Document every step, with dates, times, and quoted statements, as necessary.

- Don't promise blanket confidentiality to any employee.

- Communicate with victims or alleged harassers on a "need to know" basis.

- Use some form of progressive discipline for perpetrators in proven cases.

- Follow up with the victim(s), follow through with perpetrators(s), and monitor the situation for future occurrences.

- Model appropriate behavior for your people—what you do is often more important than what you tell people to do.

MODULE 6:
YOUR RIGHTS AS AN EMPLOYEE

As an employee, you are entitled and asked to be the "first line of defense" against sexual harassment in the workplace. This means that if you feel you are experiencing sexual harassment

- Just say "no." Let the person know you find his or her behavior offensive. This includes telling any co-worker (including your supervisor) to stop telling sexually oriented jokes, showing photos, or touching you in a way that makes you feel uncomfortable.

- If the behavior does not stop, report it to your manager (if he or she is not the offender), any other manager, and/or to Human Resources immediately.

- In more severe cases, where you believe the behavior has not stopped, you also have the right to report sexual harassment to the state or federal office of the Equal Employment Opportunity Commission.

- *You are not required to first speak with your supervisor.*

MODULE 7:
CONCLUSION

Most state laws require that

> "An Employer Must Take All Reasonable Steps
> Necessary to Prevent Sexual Harassment."

This includes having

- A *policy* expressly preventing sexual harassment, both quid pro quo and hostile environment types. This policy should define sexual harassing behavior and state that it won't be tolerated; that victims have the right to make reports without fear of retaliation; and that harassers in proven cases will be subject to discipline, up to and including termination.

- *Training* programs for managers and supervisors and awareness training for all employees.

- An *investigation* process that includes either management and/or the Human Resources Department.

- Immediate and appropriate *"corrective action"* to provide support for victims and sanctions for perpetrators.

In every workplace, sexual harassment should not be tolerated. It's about respect and responsibility. It's about productivity. And it's about the law.

SAMPLE TRAINING PROGRAM SLIDES: THE TRUE THIRTEEN

Use the text from the following slides to craft the core of your sexual harassment training program, adding or deleting as you see fit. The design will depend on the audience, length, current policies, the culture of the organization, and the (real) purpose of the program. Some of these slides can be used for a managers-and-supervisors-only program; others will fit for an all-employees training program.

The Big Picture

- Federal and state employment laws entitle everyone to a workplace that is free from sexual harassment.

- Sexual harassment is against our company policy and outside the course and scope of your employment. It will not be tolerated.

- Besides the potential for losing your job, you can be personally sued for sexual harassment.

- This is an important subject and a critical part of your employment here.

- It's about respect and dignity, personal responsibility, support for victims, and consequences for perpetrators.

Defining the Sexually Harassing or Sexually Hostile Environment

Unwanted, unwelcome, and/or repetitive visual, verbal, or physical conduct based on sex or of a sexual nature that unreasonably interferes with a person's job performance or creates an abusive atmosphere.

The New Workplace

- Business Trips, Conferences, Conventions, Sales Calls, Hotel Rooms, Airplanes, Rental Cars, Training Classes, Client Meetings

- Work-Related Lunches, Dinners, Happy Hours

- After-Work Sports Teams with Employee Members

- Company-Sponsored Events or "Approved" Parties

Sexually Harassing Relationships*

- Male to Female

- Female to Male

- Same Gender Harassment

- Harassment Based on Sexual Orientation

- Third Parties (vendors, customers)

*Remember, a boss-employee relationship does not always have to exist.

DEFINING SEXUAL HARASSMENT

- "Quid Pro Quo"—"This for that"

- "Hostile Environment"—Most common and most recognizable

- Hybrid—Combination of two types

"Quid Pro Quo"

- Job benefits connected to receiving sexual favors, typically from a supervisor, manager, director, or senior executive, who holds the power of promotion, transfer, work duties, or work schedule over the victim-employee.

- Least common form of sexual harassment—accounting for about 5 percent of reported cases in the U.S.

- Can involve female bosses and male employees, same-sex, senior executives on down to first-line supervisors.

"Hostile Environment"

- Sexually oriented or gender-based jokes, comments, photos, text, public remarks.

- Intentional rubbing, touching, or blocking the path of a person.

- Leering, ogling, flirting, looks, and gestures.

- Showing favoritism to those who allow these behaviors or reciprocate.

- No boss-employee relationship is necessary.

Bad Excuses

- The "Toucher"—"I'm a hands-on, touchy-feely kind of guy. That's just how I am. It's in my nature. It's part of my culture and my heritage. It's how we do things where I come from."

- The "Joker"—"Lighten up. I was just kidding. We're all adults here. I wasn't talking about you. I didn't mean anything by it."

- The "Looker" (a/k/a "King Leer")—"I'm trying to give you a compliment."

- The "Confider"—"I had a hot time last weekend. Let me tell you all about it. . . ."

Organizational Red Flags

- Allowing a sexualized work culture to flourish without intervention, any progressive discipline, or significant consequences for perpetrators.

- Victims who fear the consequences of reporting.

- Covert or overt tolerance by managers and supervisors, even after repeated events or reports.

- Failing to respond quickly, investigate, and stop the behavior.

The Supervisor's Investigative Process

- Respond immediately (take the complaint).

- Determine the type (quid pro quo, hostile environment, hybrid).

- Decide whether there is a policy violation.

- Identify the participants (review their files).

- Interview all participants.

- Document every step.

- Use some real form of progressive discipline.

- Follow up with victims, follow through with perpetrators, and continue to monitor.

The Employee's Reporting Process

- If you feel you have been sexually harassed, tell the person to stop the conduct, remarks, or behavior.

- If the person does not stop, report it immediately to your supervisor, another supervisor, HR, or a company senior executive.

- Don't wait until the situation escalates. Don't give the power back to the harasser by not reporting it.

- Tell the truth and provide documentation or witnesses if possible. Have patience through the HR process.

Key Management Points

- Use the "unwanted, unwelcome, and repetitive" test (severe, pervasive, interfering, intimidating, offensive).

- *Actual* (knew) *vs. constructive* (should have known) *notice?*

- Provide confidentiality, retaliation prevention.

- In "He Said/She Said" cases: Who was more likely to have said or done it? Past incidents?

- Did you take "appropriate corrective action"? Will it pass the reasonable person/organization test?

Avoiding Litigation

A successful defense involves:

- An in-place policy
- Management response training
- Continuing employee awareness
- No prior/repeated incidents
- Immediate investigative response
- Protection for victims
- Consequences for perpetrators

6

Workplace Violence Prevention Programs for Employees and Supervisors

The tendency to identify manhood with a capacity for physical violence has a long history in America.

—Marshall Fishwick

If I had the chance to do it again, I'd respond with more determination.

—Larry Hansel, convicted workplace murderer of two executives in 1991, in San Diego, California, as reported in a July 14, 2004, *USA Today* article.

Key

In reality, as a training subject, this issue is not about homicides in a corporate setting, or disgruntled postal workers, or people being killed by former co-workers. Those events are rare, overblown by the media, and off the mark from the real concern. This issue is really about *fear*, as in employees who are afraid to come to work, stay at work, do their work, or interact with a co-worker, supervisor, vendor, taxpayer, or customer. Successful training on this subject will dispel the myths about workplace violence, empower employees to report all threats or acts of violence to HR, or even the police, and create a work environment in which respect, support, and vigilance prevent this problem from ever happening.

Usual Audience

All employees for the majority of the training; managers and supervisors for a portion of it. The list of "all employees" should include all full-time and part-time workers, field and office workers, unpaid volunteers, or interns.

Best Length

The bare minimum needed to cover this subject is one hour. The maximum tends to be four hours. My usual approach is to teach all employees for three hours, then turn the frontline folks loose at that point, and train the managers and supervisors in more extensive skill-building for the last hour.

This format helps get the importance of the message to everyone at the start, and then it allows the managers and supervisors some time to talk about past incidents, current concerns, or the use of coaching, progressive discipline, or terminations as their prevention tools. I usually allow the managers to vent for a bit about difficult employee issues, previous threat cases, or domestic violence incidents that have started at an employee's home and crossed over to the workplace.

Basic Training Themes

It's best to quickly dispel two strong myths that surround this subject: that the U.S. Post Office is some kind of killing ground, and that employees should be worried about homicides happening in their workplaces. Addressing the first myth, not only does the phrase "going postal" do a huge disservice to the over 800,000 employees who work there, it's also not statistically accurate. According to an independent report from 2000, led by Joseph Califano, postal employees are no more likely to assault or kill people than any other occupation in the United States.

Addressing the second myth, most people who are injured or killed at work are doing high-risk jobs (cab driving, law enforcement, convenience store clerk), and these people are almost exclusively injured or killed by criminals who have no connection to the workplace whatsoever. If the group you are training *is not* engaged in the business of collecting money in the wee hours of the night, they are not at much risk for homicide. Most workplace violence incidents involve threats or assaults made by customers, taxpayers, vendors, passengers, patients, students, or library/park patrons, not by current or former employees.

However, if your training group is primarily female, or there is a large female contingent in the employee ranks, then you should discuss the real possibility of domestic violence (DV) issues starting at home and crossing over to the workplace. Most DV victims work, and most have been bothered by current or former partners while at work.

An Agenda slide could be made of the macro training themes for this issue:

Discuss the "New" Work Environment. Stress in the workplace; more conflicts between people; economic stress or money worries lead to violent reactions in some taxpayers, customers, employees, or recently terminated employees. Organizations that fail to treat employees with dignity during the performance evaluation, discipline, or termination process tend to have more threats or actual violence than those that are more humane and aware of the employees' stress, home issues, or money problems.

Define Violence in the Workplace Accurately. Since the year 2000, according to yearly U.S. Department of Labor studies on workplace violence, there are more than 100 million workers in the United States and fewer than 700 are killed each year at work. Most are killed by robbers, not co-workers. This issue is more about fear management than about guns in the office. Verbal threats are the most common policy violation. Management has a duty, under Occupational Safety and Health Administration (OSHA) guidelines, to provide a safe workplace, free from threats or violence. Domestic violence and stalking have now crossed over from home and become a workplace concern.

Look at Behaviors and Threats in Context. Don't use labels (crazy, scary, weird, and so forth) to describe behaviors (arguing, threatening, fighting, saying or doing certain things that a reasonable employee would see as threatening, violent, or potentially violent). Evaluate employees and others in terms of whether or not their behavior fits the context of the situation or it is clearly inappropriate.

Communication and Service Tools. Teach Communications 101 and Customer Service 101 materials here, covering how to deal with rude, aggressive, immature, preoccupied, angry, or entitled people, either as customers, vendors, or co-workers.

Personal Safety at Work. Teach the participants about reading the non-verbals and body language of potentially violent or dangerous people (violating their space, clenching their teeth or fists, not responding, suddenly staring at what they want to hit, and other signs). Teach the proper use of space and distance (social, personal, or intimate), and explain how to use proxemic barriers to their advantage (tables, counters, desks, chairs, locked doors, locked windows, vehicles, the telephone, the mail).

Current Organizational Policies

Does a workplace violence awareness and prevention policy already exist? How new is it or when was the last time it was revised? Have all employees been trained on this policy yet, or is this one of the purposes of the training?

One familiar problem with policies on this subject is when the HR folks have taken another existing policy related to employee behavior and simply substituted the phrase "workplace violence" for "tardiness" or "alcohol use." This approach usually fails on many levels, several of which have legal implications. There are many good examples of workplace violence prevention policy templates available from the Society for Human Resource Management (www.shrm.org), the American Society for Industrial Security (www.asisonline.org), or other reputable government, labor department, HR, or security-related Internet sites. No organization should seek to modify an existing policy that has nothing to do with workplace violence prevention by just adding it in.

The best policies on this subject cover several key areas:

- The definitions of workplace violence, threats, assaults, and violent acts

- Definitions of "employees" versus "customers, vendors, or patrons"

- Consequences for perpetrator-employees, including the use of progressive discipline

- Immediate suspension for egregious acts and/or termination after an investigation of the employee's conduct

- Support for potential victim-employees of workplace violence, including time off, or job, shift, or location changes

- Access to the police, paramedics; workers' compensation issues

- Access to the Employee Assistance Program

The policy should also cover the mandated requirement for all employees to report threats or acts of violence; mandated reporting requirements for all employees who have restraining orders against anyone who may come to the workplace and attempt to violate the order; and that the organization or the employee can call the local police for intervention, information, or support.

Last, any policy should address the issue of domestic violence as a workplace problem as well. This includes providing access to domestic violence resources in the community (shelter or hot line telephone numbers, brochures for social services, and other support) and language that says the organization will respond to domestic violence issues (usually with help by the police) if they affect the performance, productivity, or safety of any employee.

The Organizational Culture and Climate

It should come as no surprise that violence, as a workplace concern, tends to happen in organizations that are toxic, hostile, and confrontive in nature. The more conflicts between the employees, the more friction between the labor force and management, and the more workplace stress in general—exhibited by increased accidents, sick time, sabotage, vandalism, or arguments—the more likely the organization will experience serious incidents of threats or actual violence.

The (Real) Purpose of the Program

This is not a subject most organizations address willingly, unless there has been some type of incident, event, or litigation concern. Find out why you are there and what has gone on in the long or recent past. Many workplace violence concerns trail the participants for months or even years. Changes, or training programs, often come about only after something serious has happened.

Their Learning Keys

These include company policies, definitions, reporting procedures, the supervisor's responsibilities, sanctions for violators of the policy, protections for employee-victims, contact numbers for local police and domestic violence agencies, emergency and evacuation plans, and skill-building to help deal with angry, entitled, or hostile co-workers, vendors, strangers, or customers.

Your Teaching Keys

Focus on the realities, not statistics. Make the participants feel comfortable about an uncomfortable topic. Talk about consequences for perpetrators, including discipline, termination, or even arrest. Discuss support for victims, including access to the company EAP, time off, and job changes.

Your Success Tools

Strong PowerPoint™ slides, participant materials (which have been pre-approved by HR and/or the company attorneys), an appropriate video, some recent workplace violence examples from the media (keep in mind that 9/11 was a series of workplace violence events), a design based on understanding of the current written organizational policy, recognizing warning signs, supporting victims, stopping threatening or assaultive behaviors, and getting back to business without allowing an environment of fear to flourish unchecked.

Potholes and Sandpits

I once watched a trainer cover this subject using what I felt was a very disturbing approach. After he was first introduced, he began talking generally about the issue, and as he did, he began removing weapons (real knives, replica firearms, brass knuckles, to name a few) from his suit jacket, pockets, waist band, and other locations and placing them on the table in front of him. His point was, "These weapons may be in your workplace and you don't even know it." There was no question he had the crowd's attention, but at what cost? Most people who had attended this man's version of "training" told me that they were quite uncomfortable during this display, and still others said they were quite fearful. One woman in the group was so upset that she left at the first break and did not return.

Need I say that this is the wrong way to teach any program dealing with workplace violence? The goal is to make people *more comfortable* about an uncomfortable subject, not terrorize them. It's quite possible that there are people in the audience who have been victims of violent crime, domestic violence, stalking, or even reported or unreported acts of threats or workplace violence.

It does no good to scare people into submission. As such, be careful not to use any photos or videos that depict workplace violence with graphic images. There should never be any overt reminders of blood, sirens, guns, ambulances, injured or frightened employees, cops, or other disturbing images in any of the slides or videos. You don't want to cause any re-traumatization for past victims or plant the seeds of fear into the heads of any of the participants.

Some Fine Points

It may seem paradoxical to admit, but this subject can be covered with a fair amount of humor. Stories about people being killed at work are not funny, of course, but just because the issue is serious enough to have life or death consequences doesn't mean you have to treat it that way throughout.

In many of Hollywood's suspenseful movies, the director often calls for a moment of inserted goofiness to break the obvious tension. If you saw the movie *Jaws,* recall that after hard-edged shark hunter Quint (Robert Shaw) finished his beer while on the hunt for the beast, he crushed the can in a manly way. In the same scene, after oceanographer and Quint-nemesis Hooper (Richard Dreyfuss) finishes his coffee, he crushes the paper cup with a soft "pop." It's a great tension-breaker, and it tells us a lot about the characters. If you can find some ways to lighten the moment, to break the inherent tension attached to this tough topic, then the workplace violence training program can become memorable.

In fact, the best joke I have ever told (in terms of the biggest and longest laugh from the audience) is related—go figure—to domestic violence and the O. J. Simpson trial. I tell the group that the Simpson trial made domestic violence a national social issue. I ask them if they recall the trial and if so, who was their favorite character? I tell the rest of the joke this way:

> My favorite character was, of course, Brian "Kato" Kaelin. Everybody remember Kato? His hair, his surfer good looks, the tan, the puzzled expressions on his face when he was getting the tough questions? Well, to me, Kato Kaelin is living proof that Ginger and Gilligan may have spent at least one night together.

> (I'd like to take full credit for that joke, but I stole it from former San Diego City Attorney Casey Gwinn, one of the true pioneers in the modern domestic violence movement.)

SAMPLE LEADER'S GUIDE

FREQUENTLY ASKED QUESTIONS ABOUT WORKPLACE VIOLENCE

Use the following set of FAQs about workplace violence to help you design your own training program:

1. *Is workplace violence mostly about disgruntled ex-employees who come back to their old jobs and shoot people?*

   Ex-employees who return to their former workplaces to injure or kill other employees are a very visible part of the overall problem. This is how most media sources portray the problem, which actually makes murder at work seem more likely than it really is. However, the number of cases involving current or former employees who come to work with guns and shoot or kill people is really quite small. Statistically, in most organizations, employees are most likely to be threatened by a co-worker, not killed. Most deaths at work occur during robberies of employees by criminals.

2. *Why have we seen so many cases at the United States Post Office?*

   The USPS has had its share of tragic events involving workplace murder. However, given the sheer size of their employee population (over 800,000) and the vast number of facilities and locations where they work, the relatively small number of unfortunate incidents doesn't make the Post Office a "killing ground" or other unsafe place to work. Postal Service leaders have worked very hard to change the image of their organization and to provide many alternatives to postal employees under stress or out of control.

3. *Are "profiles" of workplace violence killers really accurate?*

   Early work in the area of workplace violence prevention focused on so-called "profile" characteristics of homicidal employees. Recent data and newer studies from government, labor, law enforcement, and security sources have changed this emphasis on personality types toward "behaviors in context" and actions by people who may be on the edge of committing violence. This approach has been far more successful in managing threats and preventing violence.

4. *What if a vendor or a customer threatens me at work? Is that workplace violence?*

   You have the right to work in a safe and secure environment, without having to worry about threats, attacks, or being injured by anyone, regardless of their connection to your organization. Cases of workplace violence threats or injuries involving former or current employees, managers, customers, or vendors will not be tolerated. These incidents will be investigated thoroughly, and the organization will take steps to discipline or terminate employees, prohibit customers or vendors from re-entering the workplace, or work with law enforcement to have any perpetrators arrested and/or convicted of crimes against the company and its employees.

5. *What are the most dangerous occupations for workplace violence problems?*

   People who work in jobs that involve cash handling, retail, security work, or transportation, especially at night, are most likely to become victims of workplace violence. According to U.S. Department of Labor workplace violence reports as recent as 2003, cab driver is still one of the most dangerous occupations in which one is likely to be killed.

6. *How many people are killed at work each year?*

   The number of fatalities due to workplace violence attacks peaked in the early 1990s at just over 1,000. As crime rates have fallen across the country, the number of deaths at work since 2000 has continued to drop below 700. While even one death is too many, this downward trend is a positive sign.

7. *Is there a "copycat" factor with some of these cases?*

   Because of extensive media coverage involving workplace violence homicides, experts in this field worry that cases that follow well-publicized events may be "copycat" behavior. This possibility calls for all employees and managers to be more vigilant about warning signs and behaviors following any significant event.

8. *I'm afraid of retaliation if I tell my boss about something I saw or heard. What should I do?*

   Although it's hard to report instances where other employees have victimized each other, or where an employee is being victimized by a non-employee (as might happen in a domestic violence issue), safety and security while at work is every employee's business. You may save a life besides your own by reporting a violation of company workplace violence policies. Meet with your boss in private or off-site, and tell him or her your concerns.

9. *How is domestic violence related to workplace violence?*

   Domestic violence often crosses over from home to work and becomes a serious workplace security issue. Perpetrators of domestic violence may or may not work with their victims at the company, but, in either case, they can make life miserable for them, their co-workers, and even the management.

   Any domestic violence incident that affects an employee's performance and productivity, or that of anyone else he or she works for or with, becomes a company issue. Management has a duty to intervene with referrals to counseling or to assist with restraining orders, police response, or home and work safety plans for all involved.

10. *Is stalking a workplace problem?*

    Like domestic violence that spills over, stalking problems can appear at work and cause many problems related to fear and poor productivity. Stalkers may be covert or known employees, strangers, or ex-spouses or partners.

    With the popularity of the Internet and e-mail among employees, stalking cases can develop across state lines or even internationally.

11. *Are restraining orders very effective?*

    Temporary or permanent restraining orders work effectively when victims work with police and the company to make sure the orders are enforced when violated by a perpetrator. These orders are not a bulletproof shield for any victim of threats or violence, but they do offer a powerful tool for law enforcement and the organization to use as part of an overall victim education and self-protection plan.

12. *I see more signs of security at our workplace. How will that help prevent problems?*

    Many firms are "hardening their targets" by making access control a top priority. By keeping unwanted people out of the company, companies can make employees feel safer. This includes the use of employee ID badges, key cards, security cameras, better lighting at night, and security guards.

13. *As a manager, how can I get my people to tell me about potential problems related to threats or violence?*

    You need to start by emphasizing the need for them to report. Create a real "open door" policy to encourage employees to report problems—sooner rather than later—to you. Use staff meetings or informal training periods to reinforce company policies and the need for employees to notify management of any potential violence issues.

14. *As a manager, why should I get involved in an employee's off-the-job problem like domestic violence?*

    Threats in the workplace make employees feel afraid to come to work and/or do their work. Fear at work involving one employee soon involves many other employees. You don't have to be a threat expert or a marriage counselor; you only have to know how and why to intervene with referrals to appropriate company resources (like the Employee Assistance Program) or domestic violence counseling or shelter services in your community.

SAMPLE TRAINING PROGRAM SLIDES: THE NECESSARY NINE

Use these slides to craft the core of your workplace violence prevention program, adding or deleting as necessary. The design will depend on the audience, length, current policies, the culture of the organization, and the (real) purpose of the program.

Defining Workplace Violence

The media says:

"a disgruntled ex-employee armed with an assault weapon. . . . "

- For our organization, it's any event involving threats, actual violence, or that:

Escalates and affects the safety and security of our employees, vendors, or customers

Damages our company property or your property

Makes you afraid to come to work, stay at work, or interact with co-workers, vendors, or customers

Starts at home and crosses over to create fear for you or others at work

OSHA Perpetrators of Workplace Violence

Type 1: Criminals or strangers.

Type 2: Customers, students, clients, patients, passengers, or vendors of the organization or its employees.

Type 3: Current or former employees.

Type 4: A current or former spouse, intimate, or dating partner.

Difficult "Customers"

- Angry or entitled customers or taxpayers
- Unpaid vendors
- Vandals or taggers
- Gang members
- Mentally ill
- Substance abusers

- Homeless
- Entitled parents
- Non-English speakers
- Teenagers
- Elderly or developmentally disabled

Potential Acts of Workplace Violence

- Threats or intimidation
- Verbally expressing a desire to hurt people
- Vandalism, sabotage, or theft
- Sexual harassment, sexual battery, assault
- Assaults or physical fights

- Domestic violence or stalking spreading to workplace
- Hate crimes
- Serious injuries from weapons or vehicles
- Suicides or attempts
- Firearms use
- Homicides

Working with the Police

- Call 911 or 9–911 from your landline phone.

- Tell the dispatcher who you are, where you are, and who is causing you or others to fear for your life.

- Describe this person's actions using behaviors, not labels. Don't say, "Some crazy guy . . . " Say what he is doing—screaming, threatening, fighting, or whatever.

- Disengage and find a safe, securable place to wait/hide until the police arrive.

Threat Management Teams

- Human Resources

- Police/Security

- Legal Counsel

- Employee Assistance Program Providers

- Mental Health Providers

- Community Agencies

- Senior Management

- Union/Labor Relations

- Threat Assessment Consultants

- Longtime Employees

The Manager's Roles and Duties

- Report any threats or violent incidents to HR and/or the police.

- Document your meetings and responses.

- Be a boss: coach, counsel, make EAP referrals, use progressive discipline.

- Follow up with victim-employees and follow through with perpetrators.

- Send two messages: (1) We care about every employee and (2) there are consequences for these behaviors.

The Courageous Employee

You must tell someone who can help:

- Your supervisor

- Another supervisor in another department

- HR, Legal, Risk Management, Safety, Facilities, Law Enforcement, EEO, or others

- One or more co-workers, who will all go with you to a supervisor or HR

What We Must Do to Prevent Workplace Violence

- Perform better pre-employment screening.

- Create new violence prevention policies, HR, safety, and security rules.

- Create a Threat Management Team.

- Provide awareness training for all employees.

- Use new intervention tools.

- Supervise employees humanely and treat them with dignity during discipline and termination.

- Don't wait for situations to get worse before we respond.

7

Substance Abuse Awareness for Supervisors

Alcohol is the anesthesia
by which we endure the operation of life.

—George Bernard Shaw

I've never had a problem with drugs.
I've had problems with the police.

—Rolling Stones guitarist Keith Richards

Key

For the typical supervisor, this subject is about as popular as the previous two—sexual harassment and workplace violence—which is to say not very. All of these topics create anxiety in most well-meaning bosses. The most common concerns are: "What do I do if I suspect one of my employees is under the influence of drugs or alcohol while at work?" or "What if I suspect something, accuse the employee, and then turn out to be wrong after I've created all this turmoil?" or "I know some of my people are using drugs. I suspect some of them might even be selling them. I'm afraid if I get involved, and they get fired, they may come after me."

Each of these concerns has merit. People who use drugs and alcohol in their personal lives to an extent where they move from use to abuse can bring these substances right into the workplace, either by choice or because of the weight of their addictions. And some of these people can become doubly desperate—to keep their jobs and manage their ever-growing addictions. They can often do one, for some unknown span of time, but not both.

Some managers and supervisors know from previous experiences with other employees that the biggest challenge to responding appropriately for them is denial on the part of the suspected employee and sometimes from senior management.

The way to teach this tough topic is to reinforce three critical themes: Trust your instincts and intuition as a boss; get help, support, and advice from HR and other peer managers; and follow the policy of your organization to the letter.

Usual Audience

The main benefit to this being a managers-and-supervisors-only training program is that it gives them the freedom to speak more freely, to bring up specific cases, past or current employees, problems related to enforcing the policy, and their general concerns in a protected environment. Without the front-line employees in the room, I see obvious signs of relief and more openness from the supervisors.

When I'm asked to teach this material to all employees, I change the content to focus mostly on two points: the dangers of chronic alcohol and drug use, in terms of the legal, medical, and social problems, and the scope of the organization's current policy. The first part provides an overview of substance abuse and the second takes all employees step-by-step through the company's response to an employee who will be tested "for-cause" under the most prevalent doctrine in U.S. business today—"reasonable suspicion" testing.

Best Length

For a supervisory audience, you can cover this topic in one to four hours, with two to three hours seeming to work best. You are not trying to turn these folks into "DREs" (Drug Recognition Experts, a court-certified designation that comes from studious training in the objective and subjective signs and symptoms of drug and alcohol use).

Your goal is to familiarize them with the policy in place, take them through the exact steps when dealing with an employee suspected of drug or alcohol use at work, and help them work effectively with HR (and in some cases, the employee's union).

If you're asked to do this program for all employees, or just the frontline people, you should be able to cover it in one to two hours, at the maximum.

Basic Training Themes

The number one drug of choice in the workplace is alcohol, followed by marijuana, then cocaine. Methamphetamine is fast becoming the illegal stimulant of choice in the workplace, soon to be more popular than cocaine, especially in California.

Depending on which studies you read, drug use among employees ranges from 8 to 12 percent of the workforce. This doesn't mean drugs and alcohol are prevalent in every single organization; statistics only offer ranges and a starting point for further investigations.

When dealing with employee symptomologies as a training issue, tell them one thing: We aren't medical doctors, so we never assume what we see is always what it will turn out to be. For example, if an employee comes back from lunch staggering, slurring his words, sweating heavily, and seeming to smell of alcohol, you would probably suspect he had had a few too many adult beverages at lunch, right? And while you may be correct, these are also the same symptoms for someone suffering from hypoglycemia or low blood sugar.

In terms of training themes, treat this issue (1) as an HR problem for managers and supervisors, (2) as a medical issue, focusing on the health of the employee, which is why we use "reasonable suspicion" testing just as much to evaluate them medically as we do to verify possible drug or alcohol use, and (3) as a legal issue, seeking to protect the employee's privacy and dignity through discreet conversations, held in private, and ultimately to protect the whole organization from the hazards of impaired employees.

Current Organizational Policies

Does a drug and alcohol policy already exist? When was the last time it was revised? Have all employees been trained on this policy yet, or is this one of the purposes of the training? Does the policy address issues around reasonable suspicion testing, post-accident testing, Employee Assistance Program use, last-chance agreements, searches of employee lockers, and interactions with the police?

The Organizational Culture and Climate

Just as you might see with the participants in sexual harassment and workplace violence programs, this subject brings out all the little jokes and smart asides from the audience. You'll likely hear, "Is this where we come to buy our drugs?" or "Are we gonna drink and give each other breath tests?" and so on.

My personal theory is that any topic that makes people think about their own past or current behavior (as past or current drug or alcohol users) leads them to try a myriad of tension-cutting jokes and comments. If you are working with a fairly young audience of managers and supervisors (age thirty and younger), there is no doubt that unless you're in a highly religious area of the country, many of the people in the training room have some drug and alcohol history that they're probably not too ready to disclose.

Some studies suggest that nearly eighty million Americans have experimented with illegal drugs. It's rare to find an adult who has not felt the effects of (way) too much alcohol at one point in his or her life. It may be possible that some of the attendees are currently battling their own demons and have a less than healthy relationship with prescription drugs, marijuana, or alcohol.

The point to all this is not to play "true confessions" and get people to disclose personal information. You simply have to be aware that you may be speaking to people who have used illegal drugs before and are uncomfortable about anyone discovering it.

While we can all agree that drug and alcohol abuse crosses all social, economic, racial, gender, and geographic boundaries, let's be real: We're more likely to find illegal drug use on the factory floor than in the executive boardroom. The guy getting arrested for drunk driving off the job is more likely to be a line employee than the head of the company. This is not to say that senior managers, highly educated people, and licensed, certified, or other professional people (doctors, attorneys, accountants, and others) don't have these issues; we know they do. However, drug and alcohol abuse is significantly over-represented in certain professions: construction, retail, fast food, and low-skill-level assembly or manufacturing positions.

Know the organizational culture when you present this material. Is this company kind of a rough-and-ready, dirt under the fingernails type of place? Is the turnover rate among the line employees high or low? Have we already seen reported incidents of fights, thefts, or arrests among the employee population? Or is the culture more oriented toward an office environment, with a strictly enforced dress code and a sense of not wanting to make too much noise in the hallways?

The (Real) Purpose of the Program

Your arrival to teach a program on the company's drug and alcohol policy will usually be driven by some event related to either substance. While some more progressive organizations simply schedule refresher training on a regular basis (usually annually), most others do it only in response to something ugly: a vehicle accident with injuries; strangers (read that as drug dealers) coming onto the property at all hours; fights; rising incidents of theft (especially big-ticket items like laptops, computer chips, tools, or forklifts); a surge in the number of anonymous reports by concerned employees; drug paraphernalia found in the employee restrooms; a medical emergency involving a drug- or alcohol-using employee; or the arrival of the police on the premises.

I trained this subject for one organization that brought me in after they had to fire over one dozen employees for failing "reasonable suspicion" drug tests.

Their Learning Keys

Existing company policies, definitions, reporting procedures, the supervisor's responsibilities, sanctions for violators of the policy, how to help the employee get access to an Employee Assistance Program, the possibility of a rehabilitation/treatment program, and return to work agreements (commonly known as "last chance" agreements, as in, "one more failed test and you'll be terminated").

Your Teaching Keys

Teach the supervisors to focus on the employee's *behaviors,* not on medical diagnoses. Have them focus on using behavior-based language, not labels. It's not correct or appropriate to write in a report, "Employee appeared drunk" or "Employee looked stoned to me." Behavior language is far more defensible: "Employee came to work with a strong marijuana smell on his person. He had red, glassy eyes and had difficulty following my conversational questions" or "I smelled the odor of an alcoholic beverage on the employee's breath. She was unsteady on her feet, she had to hold a railing as she spoke to me, and her speech was slurred."

These are signs and symptoms that any "reasonable supervisor" would perceive as potential drug and alcohol impairment. The next step is to have another peer supervisor or manager confirm your suspicions and agree that he or she sees the same behaviors in the employee.

The final step is to contact HR immediately so they can arrange to have the employee evaluated medically. An onsite company nurse would be best, but most smaller firms lack this expensive resource, so they may have a representative from security, HR, or employee/industrial relations drive the employee to a contract testing site, such as an industrial-medical clinic or a hospital.

The purpose of this is twofold: to make sure the employee is not currently in medical jeopardy (heart attack, stroke, seizures, and so forth) and to have a blood or urine sample drawn for testing. The employee is returned to his or her home or taken back to the workplace, where a responsible person (co-worker, supervisor, family member) will drive him or her home, until the results of the tests are known.

Based on a positive test, most employees are either given a chance to enroll in a drug/alcohol rehabilitation program or, if they refuse, are usually terminated.

Their return to work after a rehab program is tied to so-called "last chance" agreements, which some firms offer to provide the employee a safe return, but with stipulations that another failed test will result in immediate termination.

Teach the group that most drug/alcohol policies allow for "reasonable suspicion" searches of an employee's desk, locker, work area, or vehicle (if it's parked on designated company property). If Security is a department in the organization, a manager from there will usually conduct these searches. If not, then HR will take the lead, or ask the local police to assist. The employee may have the right to witness the search, with his or her union representative nearby as well.

A perplexing issue for the supervisors is the use of an Employee Assistance Program. They will often ask, "Can I *make* my employee go to the EAP?" The short answer is "no." You can only give the employee access to the EAP information (800 number, address, brochures, names, and other contact information) and the opportunity to call EAP and set his or her own appointment for counseling or treatment. One option that seems to work during the difficult meeting about a positive drug test is for the supervisor to literally call the EAP provider, hand the phone to the employee, and leave the room. The message is clear: Save yourself now or lose your job now.

Teach the group to call the police any time someone finds drugs or drug paraphernalia (needles, razor blades, syringe caps, spoons). These items can be potentially hazardous and should only be handled by law enforcement. Any cleaning or maintenance crews sent to these areas should already be trained in cleaning, handling, and disposal of suspected blood-borne pathogens.

Your Success Tools

PowerPoint™ slides, a participant manual (which has been pre-approved by HR and/or the corporate attorneys), an appropriate video (which is not always easy to find for this topic), some recent national or local stories from the print media perhaps, a design based on understanding of the current written organizational policy, recognizing warning signs, supporting impaired employees through a "tough love" response, and helping every manager and supervisor send the message that the use of drugs and alcohol won't be tolerated.

Potholes and Sandpits

Two potential problems exist with this type of training. One surrounds the conduct of the senior executives, who don't often attend this training, which sends the wrong message to begin with. The second comes up when the trainer tries to bond with the group by telling a few stories of his or her past, as it relates to drug or alcohol use.

Let's address the first one by reminding you to have an ally in the room. One of the primary reasons why it's more than a bit useful to have a representative from HR on hand during the training comes when a participant says, "The policy states that 'no employee will arrive or return back to work after having used illegal drugs or alcohol.' Well, I've seen the bosses drink at lunch. I've seen some of them come back looking pretty ripped. Does that mean they can do it and we can't?"

This comment is usually followed by a series of "That's right!" and "Yeah, you tell 'em, Larry!" comments from the supervisory group. (This is usually just when I start to feel the first beads of sweat form at the top of my spine.) It's a valid point. In some organizations, senior management will craft this carefully worded, legally enforceable policy and then say, "Do as we say, not as we do."

If the HR rep is sharp, he or she will step in and field this question, by saying:

> "We expect every employee, regardless of his or her position, to follow this policy. Larry, if you read it a bit further, the policy states that employees are not allowed to come to work or return to work *impaired,* whether it's from taking too many pain pills on the way back from the dentist or having a three-drink lunch. Your point is a good one. It looks like we're creating a double standard here, but we expect the senior

executives to conduct themselves appropriately, whether it's at a business lunch with clients or out of town on company business. If we discover that any employee is returning to work showing signs of impairment, which means he or she cannot do his or her job effectively, we will step in and enforce the policy."

Never, ever, ever, reveal any of your own drug or alcohol history, however brief or limited, to the group. You won't win them over by imparting this knowledge. If you say you've never been drunk or used illegal drugs (which may be the honest truth), few people will believe you. If you go the other direction and talk about your wild times, it ruins your credibility.

Some Fine Points

In their hearts, supervisors want to know they have done the right thing by intervening in an employee's life in what all parties have to agree is in a highly intrusive way. Reassure them that their instincts about an employee's impairment are usually right on, and that they are, in fact, saving the employee's life and preventing additional harm to co-workers and the organization. Like workplace violence, this subject has the potential for police involvement, arrests, and prosecution of those who sell, distribute, or possess illegal drugs.

This is not a "me" issue as a supervisor, as in, "What do I do with my employee?" It's an "us" issue, as in, "We need to respond as a management team and handle this problem together, discreetly, swiftly, and following our written policies."

To do any less sends the wrong message to employees who don't use illegal substances at work, and the wrong message to those who do.

SAMPLE LEADER'S GUIDE/ TRAINING MODULE OUTLINE

Use what you need from the following topic outline to design your own program.

MODULE 1: INTRODUCTION TO ALCOHOL AND DRUG ABUSE

Regardless of your political affiliations or beliefs about choice and civil liberties, we can all agree that the abuse of alcohol, prescribed pharmaceuticals, or illegal drugs can seriously impact the families, health, and safe working conditions of all employees. According to the National Drug-Free Workplace Alliance Web site (www.ndfwa.org):

> Most employees *do not* engage in illicit drug use, most *do not* want to work side-by-side with drug abusers, and a majority of employees are parents who are concerned about the effects of drug abuse on their children, now and in the future. Given this profile of the typical American worker, it is clear that substance-abuse prevention can and should be viewed as a common concern of both employers and employees.
>
> Drug use in the workplace costs this country billions of dollars every year in lost productivity, increased health problems and workplace accidents, to say nothing of the problems it causes us at the federal and state level with associated family problems. Contrary to the typical portrayal of drug abusers, many manage to hold down full or part-time jobs, masking their destructive problem from their employers. In fact, over 74 percent of all current illegal drug users work and over 74 percent of heavy alcohol users work (those drinking five or more drinks per occasion on five or more days in the 30 days preceding the survey).

As part of ongoing education for all employees, this organization will continue to make a good-faith effort to inform employees about the dangers of drug and alcohol use in the workplace; maintaining a drug- and alcohol-free workplace; providing information about drug and alcohol counseling, rehabilitation, and Employee Assistance Programs; and educating employees about and enforcing all penalties for drug and alcohol abuse policy violations.

Employees who use alcohol or drugs while at work, or come to work impaired, put themselves and others at enormous risk. National studies indicate nearly 8 percent of full-time employees have used illegal drugs in the past month. Chronic substance abuse at work causes a range of problems, including

- Lower employee productivity, more sick leave and absenteeism

- More employee discipline problems and terminations

- More worker injuries or deaths, especially due to accidents

- More liability exposure, increased insurance premiums, and workers' compensation costs to the company

- More property damage, theft, or loss to company and personal items, including vehicles, equipment, and money

- More employee turnover, due to the unstable, toxic, or even dangerous work environments

- Lower employee morale, caused by fear, management apathy, crimes, incidents, or accidents

MODULE 2: ALCOHOL ABUSE

While alcoholic beverages are certainly legal and part of our national fabric (inter-related to sporting events, commercial sponsorships, holidays, etc.), the problem comes when the alcohol *user* becomes the *abuser*. Recent medical studies suggest that a surprising number of people are genetically predisposed to addictive behavior, related to alcohol or drugs. As such, proponents of alcohol treatment programs believe that for those at risk for addiction, or in recovery or treatment, there is no such thing as "social drinking." As one longtime veteran of the recovery process puts it, "One drink is too many and one thousand is not enough."

The impact of alcohol abuse in our society is staggering: About 50 percent of all automobile fatalities involve alcohol and it plays a large part in domestic violence, child abuse, suicides, and violent crimes. The health risks due to the chronic use of alcohol include liver, kidney, and pancreatic disease; several forms of cancer; stomach ulcers; and diabetes.

The stages from alcohol *user* to alcohol *abuser* include

- Experimentation (drinking at an early age, testing your limits)

- Regular use (social to moderate amounts of drinking)

- Daily preoccupation (drinking becomes a large part of your life routines)

- Dependency and addiction (it negatively affects your personal and professional life and you cannot stop without help)

The main problem with this "formula" is that there is no accurate time line. Since the path to addiction varies with each person, it may take weeks, months, or even years to reach the dependency stage. At this point, however, they don't *want* a drink, they literally *need* one to survive. Once the alcohol abuser is in the grip of addiction, he or she will need to begin a supervised medical, rehabilitative, or structured recovery program to save his or her life, family, and career. Alcoholics who attempt to stop on their own either fail, get very sick, or can even die.

MODULE 3: ILLEGAL AND PRESCRIPTION DRUG ABUSE

While the concept of drugs and drug abuse makes most people think of so-called "street drugs" and images of criminals or homeless drug users, the reality is much broader and more pervasive. Drug abuse exists at every level in society and no city, county, or neighborhood is immune.

Common abused illegal (street) drugs include

- Marijuana—also known as "pot," "weed," "herb," "grass," or "chronic," this naturally grown, depressive substance is known to cause lung cancer, anxiety attacks, and depression in heavy users.

- Methamphetamine—also known as "meth," "speed," "tweak," or "crank," this chemically made stimulant powder causes mood swings, sleep disturbances, organ and brain damage, and irrational or even violent behavior in chronic users.

- Cocaine—also known as "coke," "blow," or "flake," this naturally grown and chemically processed stimulant powder causes nasal damage, heart rhythm problems, and mood swings in nearly all users.

- Opiates—including heroin, morphine, or methadone (synthetic opiate), these depressive substances are highly addictive, even after a few doses.

- Other common "street drugs"—include smoking PCP ("angel dust"); taking Ecstasy tablets ("rave" or "designer drugs"); or inhaling spray paints, thinners, glues, or solvents. Because of questionable purity and enormous toxicity, using these substances can cause brain damage, irrational behavior, and even death.

- Prescription drugs—these include pain medications, anti-depressants, anti-anxiety pills, sleep aids, and similar physician-prescribed pharmaceuticals. The issue is not the *use* of these drugs (in appropriate medicinal circumstances), but their *abuse*.

SAMPLE TRAINING PROGRAM SLIDES: THE ESSENTIAL ELEVEN

Use these slides to craft the core of your drug and alcohol awareness program, adding or deleting as necessary.

Training Goals

- Know your company's policy for drug/alcohol issues.

- Know what to do and what not to do as a supervisor.

- Send the message to all employees that it's not right to use drugs or abuse alcohol, especially at work.

- Help addicted employees help themselves, with confidentiality, access to treatment, ongoing support, and "tough love."

Substance Abuse at Work

- Reduced performance by impaired employee and others, who have to cover for him/her.

- The costs and business impacts of absenteeism.

- More conflicts, fights, and discipline.

- Potential for worker accidents, injuries, or deaths.

- Potential for liability or litigation exposure.

- Theft or damage to company or personal property.

- Higher employee turnover (good employees leave).

- Frustration by employees when management does not intervene.

Look for *Behavior Changes*

- Pay attention to employee behaviors, not just symptoms.

- Document your observations for HR.

- Get help from a peer supervisor to verify what you observed.

- Meet privately with the employee, using behavior-based language, not labels.

- Treat the issue as a safety concern, a performance concern, and a policy violation.

"Reasonable Suspicion" (a/k/a "For-Cause Testing")

- Direct observation of use, possession, or physical, objective symptoms or odors.

- A pattern of abnormal conduct or erratic work behavior.

- Arrest for drug/alcohol abuse.

- Independent, reliable sources or witnesses.

- Evidence of tampering with a previous drug test.

Drug and Alcohol Use to Abuse

- Experimentation—which either ends or escalates.

- Regular use—higher tolerances, larger amounts needed.

- Daily preoccupation with substance—where to get it, when to use it, etc.

- Dependency—a medical addiction, requiring supervised treatment to stop.

Alcohol Use at Work

Observable behaviors, signs, and symptoms:

- Odor of alcoholic beverage on breath, clothes, or person.

- Swaying movements, balance problems, slurred speech.

- Red, glassy, or watery eyes; dry mouth; flushed face.

- Difficulty holding a conversation, remembering tasks.

- Sleeps at work station, in his or her car, or fails to return to work from breaks or lunches.

- Frequent mood swings, rising anger rates, more aggressive confrontations with others.

- Frequent absenteeism without a valid medical reason.

Marijuana Use at Work

Observable behaviors, signs, and symptoms:

- Green leafy substance, most often smoked in pipes, bongs, or joints; kept in plastic baggies or small boxes.

- Acts as a depressant with hallucinogenic effects, through the chemical compound THC, which is now more potent than in the past.

- Users smell strongly of the burnt drug, on their breath, clothes, and person.

- Red eyes, hoarse cough, slowed movements, sleepiness, difficulty following a conversation, remembering tasks.

- Street names: pot, grass, weed, herb, chronic, smoke.

Cocaine Use at Work

Observable behaviors, signs, and symptoms:

- Powdered cocaine (white crystal, most often snorted) versus rock or "crack" cocaine (small chunks that have been mixed with baking soda, most often smoked).

- Strong central nervous system stimulant, raises blood pressure, heart rate, energy level.

- Users will carry the drugs in foil or paper bindles, small vials, or small baggies.

- Users will often show agitation, dilated pupils, and a runny or bloody nose.

- Street names: coke, blow, sniff, rock, crack.

Methamphetamine Use at Work

Observable behaviors, signs, and symptoms:

- Fine white powder, created in clandestine labs, most often snorted, smoked, or injected.

- A/k/a the "poor man's cocaine," due to lesser cost.

- Users will often have fidgety, nervous energy, dilated pupils, a "chemical" smell, rapid pulse.

- Chronic users almost always develop high levels of paranoia, severe skin ailments, sleep problems, and brain and organ damage.

- Street names: meth, crystal, speed, crank, tweak.

Opiate Use at Work

Observable behaviors, signs, and symptoms:

- Heroin—seen as a white or brown powder, or a brown tarry/sticky substance, carried in foil or paper bindles, tiny balloons, or plastic baggies. Most often injected, then snorted, or smoked.

- Pills or tablets: OxyContin, Vicodin, Codeine, and many others.

- Strong CNS depressant, slows the heart rate and energy level substantially.

- Heroin users will have pinpoint pupils, hooded eyelids, a runny nose, and may seek to cover injection sites with shirts, jackets.

- Pill users may have to take more and more to get the effects. Both users are at risk for overdose.

Use Your Resources

- Contact HR immediately to discuss the employee's behavior, and objective and subjective symptoms.

- Arrange for the employee to be tested and taken home.

- Contact law enforcement for issues related to drug possession, sales, searches, found narcotics, paraphernalia.

- Intervene early and send the right message to users and other employees.

8

Supervisory Training in Performance Evaluations, Coaching, Progressive Discipline, and Terminations

The best way to appreciate your job
is to imagine yourself without one.

—Oscar Wilde

Key

These are tough topics, but ones that you and the participants can really sink your teeth into. There are lots of stories (edged with humor) to tell, from both sides of the training platform, and many opportunities to use three-person role plays (boss-employee-observer) to work through sample encounters in a safe and protected environment.

Usual Audience

As with the previous chapter, these materials are best suited for managers and supervisors, as a refresher, as a continuing education or skill-building session, or as part of their orientation as new company leaders.

Best Length

In a perfect world, you would have two to three days for these programs. However, when pressed for time, you can cover these subjects in a minimum of a half-day or, at the maximum, in a full day. The full-day version should include plenty of time and space for group work, individual and group exercises, and role plays.

Basic Training Themes

One point it helps to make early is that, while the role plays will help the group members fine-tune their skills in these areas, nothing in training is ever exactly like the real thing. They can learn, laugh, and make mistakes during the role-play scenarios, but they should remember that, under the stress of the moment, they will have to use their past experiences, common sense, and intuition to get through some of these real-time employee encounters successfully.

It's important to remind the group that no matter how tough or stressful these meetings seem for them as the bosses (especially at the hard end of the behavioral spectrum—hostile discipline and terminations), they are doubly difficult for the employees. They realize these sessions have much more tension or urgency attached to them because bosses hold the power of their promotion, pay, duties, responsibilities, or even their continued employment, in their hands.

As a result, there are three possibilities for the more difficult meetings: The employee will sit sullenly and pout throughout the session, only agreeing to some points and not others; the employee will debate, argue, and challenge every point, raising the emotional temperature in general and your blood pressure in particular; or the employee will nod and agree and say, "You're absolutely right. I need to do that and I will." For this last type, the meeting ends and you think to yourself, "I'm a genius. I'm the best supervisor on the planet," only to discover later (after no change is evident) that the employee simply agreed with you just to get out of the room as quickly as possible.

Having conducted or attended a number of these high-stress or even high-risk meetings, I know that a sticking point for most supervisors happens at the moment during the meeting at which the employee simply refuses to acknowledge the presenting problem. This can lead to conversations we all used to have in the schoolyard:

> **You:** "After reviewing your attendance records, I wanted to speak to you about getting to work on time."
>
> **Hostile Employee:** "I don't have an attendance problem."
>
> **You:** "Do so."
>
> **Hostile Employee:** "Do not."
>
> **You:** "Do so." And so on, and so on, and so on.

There are four training keys to help supervisors prevent this circular dead-end.

Always Focus on Behaviors, Not Labels

Don't say, "You're always late," which is a label. Discuss the late-arriving or poor-attendance-related behaviors, for example, "On Monday you were 15 minutes late. On Tuesday you were 30 minutes late." Don't say, "You're not a good team player," which is a label. Say, "I've noticed that when it gets busy, you don't help your co-workers with the group projects and deadlines you're all responsible for."

Always Speak from a Position of Proof

Use either data or direct observation, rather than from speculation or guessing. The proof lies in the numbers, or what my father calls "the intra-ocular impact test," that is, what hits you between the eyes. Pull the attendance rosters; pull copies of e-mail where the employee promised something and didn't deliver; and pull the production numbers, sales figures, or work orders. And direct observation means something you saw or that was reported to you by a reliable source (peer manager, your boss, a trusted subordinate with no hidden agenda against the employee).

Always Keep Moving On with the Meeting

Keep going, even if the employee refuses to see there is a behavioral or performance issue. I've seen supervisors play the "did not/did so" game for 20 minutes. I've seen others stay stuck on Step 2 of the Discipline Model (see the slides for more details), unwilling and unable to move forward until the employee finally agrees, "Yes, you're right. I missed my sales numbers for this quarter." If the employee refuses to see the issue from your perspective, save yourself the aggravation by putting on the hat that says, "I'M THE BOSS," and saying, "I'm sorry you don't agree. I feel it is an important issue and, as your supervisor, I'm going to ask you to stop the behavior or fix the problem. Here's what solutions I see for this. . . ." Move on to the next step in the discipline process from there. (To train this material even more effectively, read Dick Grote's epic book on this issue: *Discipline Without Punishment* [AMACOM, 1995].)

Always Return the Focus Back to the Employee

How do you answer these accusatory questions from the employee: "How come you never talk to Leslie about her attendance problems? Why are you always picking on me about coming in a few minutes late?" With this: "I'm not picking on you and I will address Leslie's issues later. We're talking about you, not her, so let's go back to what we were discussing. . . ." Keep redirecting the focus back to the employee's issues, not other people. Don't get distracted by side conversations that the employee initiates to cloud the main problem.

Current Organizational Policies

Add copies of the company policies for performance evaluations, progressive discipline, and terminations to your handouts. Have HR approve your training design and handouts before you proceed.

The Organizational Culture and Climate

Some companies take away most of the power to solve their subordinates' problems by telling supervisors to speak to HR before they do anything related to investigating, solving, or stopping employee behavioral problems.

Other companies take a more hands-off approach, empowering their leaders to confront and manage their own issues, and only come to HR for guidance when the problem exceeds their experience, expertise, or authority. From a training perspective, it will help you greatly to know which is which where you are working. Otherwise, you could spend a lot of time teaching managers and supervisors to get involved in things their HR department does not want them to touch under most circumstances.

As an example, some firms ask their managers and supervisors to contact HR immediately if one of their people makes a sexual harassment complaint. At that point, HR will take over completely, interview the parties, review past documentation and any existing evidence, and make a decision as to any discipline, victim support, punitive or group training, and so on.

In this same situation, other firms ask their managers and supervisors to handle the claim themselves, investigate the issues, interview the parties, even suggest the appropriate discipline, if any, and, as one HR director puts it, "Bring the whole case to us with a nice bow on top and let us have it from there."

I understand the need for the first approach; we want our managers and supervisors to do the right thing, get expert HR/labor law guidance right away, and let those who know the company policies best handle it legally and effectively. On the other hand, I also see the need to let bosses be bosses and not have them run to HR every time there is a blip on their departmental radar screen. The first approach teaches managers and supervisors to defer, not trust their instincts and experience, and wait for HR to ride to the rescue. This process will start to fail as the company grows and HR gets too busy to respond immediately. A backlog of serious cases (sexual harassment, workplace violence, threats, discrimination, or other employee behavioral issues) where HR is slow in responding is bad for everybody's business.

The (Real) Purpose of the Program

There are three: help the managers and supervisors write effective, defensible, and accurate performance evaluations; help them to confront and solve continuing behavioral or performance problems with their people (the coaching and progressive discipline piece); and help them handle the most difficult HR issue of all, safe and legal terminations.

Their Learning Keys

Company policies, definitions of HR terms, reporting procedures, and the supervisor's responsibilities.

Your Teaching Keys

Here are four core "macros" to help you train these HR subjects. Use these as primary discussion points as to how and why we involve ourselves in employee behavior and performance issues, good and bad.

"Firm, Fair, and Consistent." This is more than just a slogan; it should become an operating style for the HR department and all managers and supervisors. This approach—these words—are what every employee expects, wants, and demands from bosses and from the company. These terms, and the foundation that they are supposed to represent, have a history in the labor union movement. This is how the unions expect management to treat their members. This is the language new and veteran managers and supervisors can use in group and individual meetings, to set their standards for performance and behavior; for example, "My approach is to treat every employee the same: firmly, fairly, and consistently. This will give you a better idea of what I expect from you and what you can expect from me."

"Business Impact." This is a great phrase to use for those difficult performance evaluation, counseling, coaching, discipline, and termination meetings. This concept says to all employees, "We will get involved, with a coaching, discipline, or termination response, when what you do *impacts the business* of this department or company in a negative way. Conversely, we will provide rewards, recognition, and promotions when what you do *impacts the business* in a positive way." This phrase is also quite useful in those testy meetings where the employee shouts, "You're just saying these things because you don't like me. In fact, you've never liked me!" As a supervisor, a good response is, "No. This problem has nothing to do with my personal feelings toward you. It's a *business impact* issue. What you have been doing—showing up late, taking and making personal calls throughout the day—hurts the business of this department. When other people have to cover your work *and* do theirs, it hurts this business."

"Consequence Behavior." Another great phrase to use in individual and group meetings to set early standards or explain why you must take certain HR or discipline-related actions. If the employees don't think that consequences exist, then they will continue their negative behavior unabated. The message from HR and the managers and supervisors should be: "There are consequences for these behaviors. When you do them, and when you violate our policies, you can expect to bear the consequences, up to and including discipline or termination."

Point of View. Sometimes it's hard for veteran supervisors to remember what it was like to be a new, a struggling, or an anxious employee. Sometimes it helps the boss to put himself or herself into the shoes of the employee and see things from his or her *point of view.* This is useful in answering the "why" question for certain employee behaviors or performance problems. Is it an off-the-job issue? Is the employee angry at someone or me? Does he or she need more support, different duties, a goal-setting session, or a job change? It helps the supervisor to live in the employee's world and see things from his or her perspective, if just to clarify the possible reasons, the next steps, or the most effective response.

For an outside trainer, teaching the participants about writing successful performance evaluations is complicated by the fact that you may not have much experience with their reporting forms. Every company uses a different version and, like many training feedback sheets, a lot of them are poorly designed. It helps to have pre-training meetings with HR to get some guidance and sample templates of what has worked best.

One way to teach coaching skills might be to hold a special seminar for a selected group of managers and supervisors, HR generalists or specialists, or internal OD consultants to provide them with the tools necessary to go out and serve as internal coaches in the company. This full-day seminar should provide a set of coaching tools, an overview of self-assessment instruments to use with the coachees, some typical coaching interventions, and how to provide coaching support to willing versus unwilling employees.

True progressive discipline (PD) is a flexible process, not a carved-in-stone set of edicts. Remind the participants that they can skip steps in their company's PD policy. If the employee's behavior is egregious enough, they can suspend this person on the spot. Do we need proof? "Now, Larry, I'm not going to tell you again about bringing that gun to work. One more time and I'm gonna have to write you up."

Managers and supervisors should know they have the right, the ethical duty, and the authority to take bold steps before the situation gets worse or someone gets hurt. While we don't fire people on the spot anymore, we do initiate immediate suspensions for serious policy violations: sexually touching a co-worker, assaulting a customer, stealing, fighting, selling drugs, and that sort of behavior. We can always terminate the employee after we and/or HR has conducted an investigation and made a business decision when the emotional temperature is back down.

As an exercise in discussing the termination process, ask the managers and supervisors to put themselves into the shoes of the terminated employee. Extract from the group a list of easel pad pages that describe the possible thoughts, feelings, and emotions that the employee might feel during these events. When the whole group feeds their lists back to each other, this form of perspective-taking can be helpful, especially for those bosses who forget or dismiss the absolute emotionality of these situations for the soon-to-be-ex-employee.

My experience has shown me that once an employee suddenly and finally realizes he or she is being fired for performance or behavior reasons, his or her *primary* concern is getting another job. The *primary fear* is that you and/or the organization will "black ball" him or her by providing a negative reference. Because this is the ultimate distraction, the person may not hear or listen to anything you or the HR people say during the meeting, in terms of last pay checks, continuing benefits, vacation hours, and so forth.

Therefore, teach the group to decide on the employee's reference question strategy *prior* to the termination meeting. I often provide the terminated employee with an absolutely generic "reference" letter (which is not a reference letter in reality) that simply provides any perspective employer with the former employee's name, date of hire, date of separation, duties, and/or last pay grade. This does not harm the company in any way; it simply verifies what the former employees will be putting on their resumes or applications and mirrors what we would say if the employer called HR to verify these facts.

Your Success Tools

Strong PowerPoint™ slides, videos on performance evaluation, handling coaching or discipline meetings, strong role-play scenarios, and support and approval from the company HR department.

Spend some time developing well-crafted, dynamic, and realistic role-play scenarios in these key areas: performance evaluation discussions with less-than-pleasant employees; coaching, as a pre-discipline event, with an employee who has made some mistakes; progressive discipline, where the employee must sign a written warning; and a termination of an employee.

Practice good wordsmithing on these role plays; make sure they have enough meat to give the "actors" (the manager and the employee) enough to do. If you hear from the group: "That would never happen here" or "That doesn't seem like what he or she would say in this situation," then you've not written a good case study.

Potholes and Sandpits

Don't let the role plays get out of hand, either with too much heat between the participants (it's easy for them to get carried away when acting out the parts) or by allowing lethargy from the participants (don't let them fake their way through the scenarios). Tell the three-person groups to spend about 5 to 10 minutes per scenario, ask the "observers" to give both parties some feedback, get them to switch roles, and become a new player (or observer) in the next scenario. It may help to take the observers from each group aside briefly and ask them to keep track of the time, provide specific feedback to the other two parties, and referee the scenarios, if necessary.

Some Fine Points

Some people define the acts of "coaching" and "counseling" as if they were the same. I see them differently, and I think the semantics are important. To me, the concept of counseling covers two distinct issues, one not so positive and one positive. I use *counseling* as an early warning for progressive discipline. As managers and supervisors, we can intervene with a relatively "friendly" conversation that says, "Here's what I've been seeing, in terms of your work performance or work behavior. I wanted to give you a chance to tell me what, if anything, is going on and how I can help. This is not a formal warning, but it could become one if we have to revisit these same problems later."

The more positive aspect of counseling relates to career development. In this format, we use counseling to help and support employees with their educational goals, career advancement, and to seek opportunities inside and outside the organization. Here, the focus is on the long-term and using the various resources to provide employees the chance to grow. One frustrating part of this version is that some managers and supervisors can't understand why some employees seem rather nonchalant about their bosses' efforts to help them advance. Why? Because some employees are perfectly happy where they are and may not welcome the move out of their comfort zones.

From a training perspective you can either teach the coaching process as the precursor to progressive discipline or as the career-builder piece, if you have the knowledge or the organizational resources, that is, specific programs from the training department, budget money to send people to outside development programs, or whatever it takes.

COACHING SKILLS FOR SUPERVISORS' LECTURETTE

Selecting the right person for the right job
is the largest part of coaching.

—quality guru Philip Crosby

Change, in most areas of our lives, is driven by events. We change our eating, smoking, or exercise habits only after a significant health scare. We put an alarm system in our homes or cars only after a burglary or a break-in. We became focused on air travel safety and passenger/luggage screening only after the tragic events of 9/11. Products are recalled after an injury or death; grates or safety railings go up after someone has fallen; and organizations make changes, through training, new policies, or updated procedures, only after the threat of litigation, bad publicity, or a class-action settlement.

As a coach, I most often am called to help in situations in which the person in question has sexually harassed a co-worker or subordinate; victimized others with yet another angry outburst; or somehow violated the boundaries of the organization for the umpteenth time. The work I do in these events could be called "career rescue," because the organization has had it with the employee in question and he or she is quite close to termination.

And yet, senior management (often driven by the HR office) holds out hope that, if I can succeed in changing the employee's behavior, they can salvage the relationship, the position, and the quality of the employee's work product or performance. One of the ironies of these circumstances is that the quality of these employees' work is often quite good, as they are often excellent salespeople, programmers, engineers, or whatever, but are plagued with either a terrible personality, a complete lack of social intelligence, or both.

At this stage and as a management subject, the coaching process has too much mystery surrounding it. It's not about helping employees find their "inner" selves; it's about providing them with useful tools for improvement, solving behavioral problems, and helping them move ahead with their careers. Too many people involved with coaching, internally and externally to the organization, think they can "fix" everybody, regardless of their issues.

This rarely works and, what's worse, they think more sessions are better. Coaching is not a car wash—"dirty" employees going in one end of a closed system and coming out "clean" at the other. Coaching is not psychotherapy; it's about matching the right coach for the right employee and working together on a well-defined process for skill building. And coaching, at least in a business setting, is not about helping the employee take a "spiritual journey of self-discovery."

The new landscape of coaching has succeeded in dividing itself into two "armed camps": one, the "life coaches," who help people develop greater creative, spiritual, or even neo-cosmic insight into themselves and, two, "executive, management, and employee-level coaches," who tend to focus on either strategic improvement, career skills, or management development, or problem fixing for employees who are in career jeopardy.

Neither side thinks the other has much of a handle on the coaching process, with the former group seeing the latter as lacking humanistic compassion and too focused on outcomes and efficiencies, and the latter seeing the former as flighty, too superficial, and not solution-focused enough to be taken serious by senior management.

For senior management buy-in, we need to apply proven coaching success tools (like assessment instruments, goal setting, and behavior modification) that can demonstrate to senior management that there has been progress, improvement, and that they will see the "new and improved" employee as a result of the intervention.

From my perspective, there are four dimensions for a coaching intervention:

- *Category 1: Strategic*—for senior executives; the focus is on the long-term direction of their business, department, or career goals.

- *Category 2: Developmental*—for managers and supervisors; the focus is on problem solving, managing their "Bug List," employee supervision issues, team or individual conflicts, delegation, time management, and stress management.

- *Category 3: Corrective (a/k/a "career rescue")*—for managers, supervisors, and employees who "don't get it." The focus is on helping them understand the negative impact of certain behaviors on their jobs and with others, then helping them to comply, change, or stop them. Issues include anger management, sexual harassment, micro-managing, or aggression.

- *Category 4: Special*—for high-risk HR cases involving on-the-job or off-the-job threats to employees or the organization.

My experience suggests that these coaching interventions are almost always *driven by one of these events:*

- A sharp downturn in the business success of the department or the organization

- The failing "mental health" of the executive level or departmental management teams

- Topped-out career advancement problems with certain apathetic employees

- Departmental conflicts between work groups and related team performance problems

- Employee behavioral issues related to compliance problems (sexual harassment, anger management, off-the-job concerns spilling over to work, suspicion of drugs and alcohol use)

- Angry/threatening employees

For managers and supervisors who want or need to get involved in the coaching process, it helps to see it as a preemptive, proactive tool, rather than a reactionary tool.

SAMPLE TRAINING PROGRAM SLIDES: THE ESSENTIAL ELEVEN

Use these slides to help build the core of your program.

Performance Evaluation Tips

- Employees should never be surprised about their evaluations. If so, you're not discussing their work or work habits often enough.

- Write the hard ones first, when you're more motivated to create accurate, detail, and goal-oriented reports.

- Never just leave it with the employee. Always have a meeting to discuss the results.

- Even your shining stars can develop new skills.

- Give your employees their copies, even if they say they don't want them.

Performance Evaluation Discussion Steps

1. Start the meeting with a brief overview of the evaluation, then allow time for the employee to read it.

2. Describe success areas first, then the problem areas, then the opportunities for skill improvement.

3. Help the employee develop viable solutions.

4. Get a commitment from the employee to keep, stop, or start doing certain behaviors or tasks.

5. Discuss a performance improvement or a career development plan. Set deadlines or benchmarks together.

6. End the meeting after you've answered all questions.

How/Why to Use Coaching

- As Part of an Integrated HR Strategy

- As a Highly Focused Development Option

- To Stay Connected with Key Performers

- As a Targeted Intervention for Critical Incidents

Targeted Coaching

1. *Executive/Strategic Coaching:* senior leaders, strategic issues, top team

2. *Developmental Coaching:* leadership, management, personal skills

3. *Corrective Coaching:* career "rescue," skills deficit, compliance issues

4. *Special-Purpose Coaching:* special skills, special issues, high-threat situations

The Coaching Program

Critical Success Factors:

- Dual Value: Individual and Enterprise

- Linked to Business Mission, HR, OD Priorities

- Leverages Business Results

- Cumulative, Developmental

- Confidential and Apolitical

The Coaching Experience

Critical Success Factors:

- Motivated Client

- Competent Coach

- Relationship That Builds Rapport

- Reliable Coaching Process and Model

- Outcome-Oriented Process

Coaching Methodology

- Comprehensive Personal Assessment

- Individual Development Plan (IDP)

- Action Learning Process

- Cognitively Based

- Tailored Coaching Experiences:

    Developmental

    Issue-focused

    Corrective

Progressive Discipline:
A Flexible Continuum, Not a Lock-Step Plan

- Early-warning counseling or coaching

- Verbal warning(s)

- Written warning(s) (actual number depends on HR policy)

- Suspension, with or without a performance improvement plan

- Demotion, transfer, shift change

- Termination

A Discipline Model

1. Open the meeting with a description of the behaviors or performance areas that need improvement.

2. Ask for agreement from the employee that these issues need improvement. Whether you get it or not, move to Step 3
   (Assert yourself, "I believe they do. . . .")

3. Ask the employee for new ways to solve the issues from Step 1. Provide your own solutions if necessary.

4. Get or assign a starting date for these improvements to begin.

5. End the session with a recap of what was discussed and agreed on. Set a follow-up meeting date.

Termination Process

- Practice humane management, even if you have to suppress your true feelings. Respect the employee's feelings as valid for him or her, at that moment.

- Get to the point quickly; don't be vague.

- Allow the person to talk, vent, or ask questions.

- Provide the employee with a plan you both agree on for handling reference calls from prospective employers.

Termination Process (continued)

- Don't dwell on past sins. Tell the person he or she is being let go for business or performance reasons, not "an attitude problem."

- Don't provide a false hope of taking another job in the company.

- Establish a single point of contact (usually HR) for any post-termination questions.

- Stick to your decision. It's not a negotiation.

9

Conflict Resolution
Reaching Teams and Groups Under Stress

*[About a particularly argumentative riverboat pilot
he worked under] He did his arguing with heat . . . and
I did mine with the reserve and moderation of a subordinate
who does not like to be flung out of a pilot-house
that is perched forty feet above the water.*

—Mark Twain

Key

Like other tough training topics, this subject is as event-driven as it gets. I've yet to see an HR department or a client bring me in when everyone is getting along fine. I have worked with successful, high-performing, or cohesive teams, but in those situations, the program is usually called "Team Building," and not "Conflict Fixing." The very heart of the issue—resolving conflicts between teams or work groups—suggests that people haven't been playing well with others.

The larger problem with the event-driven nature of group conflict is that the damage has been ongoing, not for just a few months, but often, for years.

It's not unusual to arrive on the scene to discover that certain employees have been angry at each other for *decades!* I've seen the less-than-pleasant results that come from five years of the silent treatment. While we'd like to believe that rancor of this magnitude is the result of some heinous crime—infidelity with a co-worker's wife, stealing a prized possession and selling it on the Internet, or worse—it's mostly about stupid things, for example, "He refused to shake my hand after a meeting seven years ago" or "I heard she said some terrible things about me eighteen months ago."

It doesn't matter if the wounds are old and scabbed or fresh and raw, if the conflict among one or more of the group members is mostly based on some previous sin/personality clash, then you are all in for a long training day.

Three pieces of advice apply: (1) Do your research on each team member, via individual interviews with them prior to the training day, and through in-depth conversations with the department heads. (2) Get some help; this subject is best taught/facilitated in pairs. Find a good partner to watch your back. (3) Be ready for anything: tears, shouts and screams, table-pounding, threats to fight outside, people storming out, and after it's over, some people may lose their jobs, either because they will be unwilling to change their negative behavior or because the conflict has escalated out of control.

Usual Audience

Angry people. Anxious people. Outspoken people, who plan to say a lot. Fearful people, who don't plan to say a word. Groups that have had a long history with each other (in some industrial settings or in public works departments, it's not uncommon for the "rookie" of the group to have twenty-five years on the job). Groups that have many veteran members who are in conflict with the newer team members, or vice versa, where the younger ones outnumber the older workers and there is conflict about how each side does its jobs.

There's one important issue you'll need to address about the group dynamics, and that is the presence of the group's supervisor or department head. Should this person attend the training sessions or not? It's a critical concern because sometimes, *he or she* is the principal reason for the conflict, in the group's perceptions, because of his or her managership or leadership style. In other cases, the frontline supervisor gets along with the group, but his or her boss does not, or vice versa, where the director or the department head (being at an arm's length to the group's day-to-day efforts) gets along fine with the employees, but the frontline supervisor is perceived as the problem.

You'll usually learn this information during the one-on-one interviews with each employee. Some of the more brusque employees will tell you, "If our boss is there, I'm not coming" or "If our director shows up, I'll guarantee you right now, no one will say a word."

As such, telling the supervisor or department head that his or her presence may be detrimental to the problem-solving, conflict-reduction process is no fun. It's one of those hard yet crucial conversations you'll need to endure to make certain you can get any results during the session. I have found that some supervisors are visibly relieved to hear it's best they don't attend, while others pout about it. In either case, I've already told each team member that what we talk about during the training session is *not* confidential (except outside the team or work group membership itself), so I will be sharing what we learn, discover, and solve with the missing supervisor or department head anyway.

Best Length

This program works best when it covers a specific span of time, ranging from several days of work to monthly follow-ups. My usual model is to first meet with the supervisor(s) and the department head, to get the scope of the problem and have them pinpoint the problem people (at least from their perspective) for me. Next, I schedule a series of 30-minute private interviews with each team member. I tell each employee that, while I'm not a priest or a psychologist, I will agree to keep what he or she tells me as confidential (providing it's not an active violation of company policy or state law). During the training sessions, I focus on the general themes of the group's conflicts anyway, not specific information revealed to me by employees during the interviews.

At the conclusion of each interview, I may (or may not, depending on my take on the group dynamics) give each employee a self-assessment instrument

(Mindex, I-SPEAK, 16 PF, Social Intelligence, Predictive Index, DISC, or some other one) and ask him or her to complete it prior to the start of the training session. During the training, I usually ask the group to share their individual scores or results and we talk about differences, similarities, and how work and personality conflicts arise just from the differing ways people see the world.

Once I've completed the employee interviews, I'll reconvene with the supervisor(s) and department head for one last debriefing before the training session the next day.

The training session itself is usually scheduled for one full day of work and then a half-day debriefing session the very next day. After the half-day program, I'll get the group to agree to meet again with me for a half day, in about thirty days, and then again for another half day in about six months. These follow-up sessions can serve as a good indicator of the success of the intervention.

Basic Training Themes

Besides the pre-training work and the multi-session design, the underlying themes of this topic are confronting poor performance and confronting the problems, events, incidents, rumors, gossip, or historical bad blood that has been holding back all or certain members of the group.

A critical and repetitive theme is the early creation of a list of "ground rules" that you will extract from them and they will promise, in the form of an oral, behavioral "contract" among all of you, to follow and enforce with each other, throughout the sessions, and into the future.

Examples of ground rules include "listen fully and don't interrupt the other person until he or she is finished speaking"; "no side conversations"; "no shouting or disrespecting anyone"; "no insults or personal attacks"; "ask clarifying questions before you make assumptions or value judgments"; "you must give direct, personal feedback to the other person, not to the group or the facilitator; by making eye contact with the other person and talking right to him or her."

These seem obvious until the session deteriorates and participants forget all the rules. You must develop the shorthand, coded phrase of "Folks, ground rules!" to keep them from attacking each other, and ask them to use it with each other. You know you're making progress when certain group members start to admonish the group, "People! Ground rules!"

As the session starts to develop momentum, it's likely one or more "alpha leaders" will emerge and try to take control. Use them as "question levers" (like verbal crowbars) to help you pry/extract the real reasons you're all here from the rest of the members, for example, "Dave, you seem like you've been here a while. Please tell us what happened last month that started the silent treatment between everyone."

You can also refer them back to the pre-training interviews by bringing up some general themes, past problems, and conflicts (without revealing exactly who said what or about whom). This can start a process of accusations and counteraccusations, so you have to be ready to intervene, keep them focused on results over emotions, and keep to the agreed-on ground rules while you work.

When the *real* issue comes out, don't sweep it back under the rug. Let the water boil enough so that the problem can take full shape, other people can see how it has hurt one or more group members, and so the group members can provide feedback about it. (One of your roles is to poll the group and get them to tell each other how the problem has impacted or hurt them, if at all. Some sagas took place long before other employees were hired.)

One advantage of airing problems that seemed horrific way back when is that they can seem sort of ridiculous or comical when discussed rationally by the group as a whole. Some members will usually realize this sooner than others and ask why the affected people spent so much time obsessing about it.

Don't forget the power of ceremony. I have had good success by simply getting the warring parties to shake hands and call an end to the hostilities. I have asked one person to sincerely apologize to the other person, or the group, or to ask the group to forgive co-workers and/or "accept" them back into the group. Human beings affiliate, meaning they have a strong tendency to do things together, and for the good of the group.

Current Organizational Policies

Every company should have a policy that says, "Get along with each other. Check your problems at the door. Respect each other's differences. Follow the instructions of your boss and try to create good work every day." None do, that I know of, because those policy statements might work well for robots or computers, but not so well for human beings; so conflict becomes inevitable. Some companies have policies that reflect the need for people to treat each other humanely, with dignity, and with respect, but the issue of how to resolve interpersonal conflicts is not often addressed.

The Organizational Culture and Climate

The concept of the toxic workplace versus the nourishing workplace applies here. Toxic organizations breed hostility, anxiety, and angst among the workers. They can't take it out on their bosses directly (see Chapter Six when they do), so they attack each other, and usually in childish, passive-aggressive ways. Toxic organizations are even worse when the managers and supervisors are perceived by the employees as toxic as well (micro-managers, harsh, abusive, distant, game-playing, credit-seeking, sabotaging, harassing, unavailable bosses). All of this makes the ground fertile for sowing seeds of discontent.

Nourishing organizations seem to be exemplified by the old adage, "We work hard here and we play hard here." There is accountability for good results, people have to work cohesively to succeed, but they also take care of their folks. There is management-employee peace (the labor unions or employee associations are viewed more as partners than adversaries) and they try to make this a place where people can stay as long as they want to, providing they do the jobs they're paid for. These places tend not to have nearly as much conflict (or it's not as severe, pervasive, or as long-lasting), either between employees or teams, because it's seen as bad for business by all concerned.

When I discuss this toxic-nourishing concept in Supervisory 101–type classes (adding in a bit of Douglas McGregor's Theory X—employees are unmotivated and lazy—versus Theory Y—employees can be motivated through empowerment), some newer supervisors say, "I'm not in charge of the whole company. I just supervise one little department. How can I have any impact?"

The question they're really asking is this, "Can I create an island of nourishment (my department) in a sea of toxicity (the rest of the company)?" I believe the answer is yes, that you can make your department, your team, your workers, a place where your people don't want to leave and other outside employees are clamoring for a spot there, just so they can enjoy what they hear their co-workers have been getting—adult, respectful, humane, and accountable treatment by each other and by the supervisor.

The (Real) Purpose of the Program

Sometimes the goal will be to get the team out of an immediate (acute) crisis mode and back to something that resembles full productivity. For other situations, the goal will be to seek out and solve long-term (chronic) problems that have been plaguing the group and its members for years.

Their Learning Keys

Your training message for their learning should be threefold: We will get to the bottom of what is keeping us from speaking or working together; we will learn new ways and new rules to treat each other with respect; and we will put these practices in place into the future.

Your Teaching Keys

One advantage of the pre-training interview work is that, on the day of the program, the team is not meeting you cold, for the first time. Hopefully, you will have had a chance to build some degree of rapport with most of them. It's important that you do what you can to position yourself as a facilitator, an interested participant, but one who is not caught up in the politics or emotions of whatever the conflict is about, so you can provide a top-down perspective.

You should start with a discussion of goals of the day:

- What makes any team successful and what makes them perform poorly?

- What are some characteristics or highlights of the best team you ever worked for, and what was the worst team and why?

- What "ground rules" can we develop together, today, to use now and into the future?

- Can we discuss what has been holding back this group?

- Can we agree to get back together tomorrow, in thirty days, and in about six months, to check on our collective progress?

Your Success Tools

PowerPoint™ slides, handouts, easel pads, marking pens, tape, and—no kidding—boxes of tissues in case the flow of tears becomes an issue.

Potholes and Sandpits

Don't back down or away from the trouble and strife when it arises. These problems have been boiling below the surface for years. Shoving them back below does no good and ignores the reason they asked you to facilitate in the first place. In these types of sessions, anger and accusations often need to come out. As long as no one hits anyone, you should be okay. Emotions can only run hot for so long; people cannot vent forever!

Continue to reinforce their need to follow the group's agreed-on ground rules, but let them vent. It may take seven hours of "Everything's fine. We don't have any issues. We don't know why you're here," until the bubble finally bursts and it all hits the table at hour eight. This is a normal part of the process; human beings swim away from conflict and confrontation as hard as they can paddle.

Don't end the session on a bad note. Even if you plan to reconvene the next morning at that exact spot in the materials or in the conflict-resolution process, try to get all the parties to shake hands (literally) and call a peace treaty until the next day.

Some Fine Points

Work with a partner you can trust and whose training style meshes with yours. This kind of training intervention can be draining, physically and emotionally. You need an ally who has experience in this area; this is not for the novice trainer.

There is a good chance that the people who have the most problems working in the group may also be on very thin ice, in terms of their continued employment. It's not unusual for one or more historically difficult people to practice "ballistic podiatry." In other words, they shoot themselves in the feet during the session.

I have returned the next day to find one or more group members had quit, been terminated, or tried to file a workers' compensation stress claim (using the training session as the final straw). I have returned in thirty days to find half the group gone through job transfers, reassignments, demotions, terminations, or voluntary resignations.

I'm not being flippant with people's lives or their careers when I say that to perform true conflict *resolution* (where you actually make progress, solve longstanding problems, and teach new ground rules for success), you must make an omelet. To make an omelet, you're going to have to break a few eggs. Some people may not survive this process, through their own headstrong choices, or when management sees a perfect opportunity to thin the employee forest of some longstanding dead wood.

THE CONFLICT RESOLUTION LECTURETTE

Conflict costs money. It's bad for business along many levels: the people side of the enterprise; the productivity, morale, and team cohesion; and the simple fact that employees who don't like coming to work in a toxic environment will quit.

It may be no surprise that many of the employee-driven arguments, anger, or long-running versions of the "silent treatment" actually stem from small problems that grew over time, were allowed to fester, and remain unresolved. I've seen a disagreement over who refills the office coffee pot turn into a major, two-sided battle, lasting many months.

YOUR CONFLICT RESOLUTION TOOL BELT

No professional construction worker or auto mechanic would try to build or fix anything without the proper tools. Yet, how many business people enter "repair" situations lacking the correct tools for the job?

Start by teaching and modeling good communication ground rules. If you're the group leader, the employees will look to you in most situations involving conflict. The behaviors you display during any group or two-person mediation session will go a long way toward determining the success, now and in the future. Simply using the phrase, "Hey, folks, remember our ground rules," during those moments when the heat in the room rises, can bring the participants back to a manageable level.

Here are some good "ground rule tools" to help minimize office conflict situations:

- *Describe people in terms of their behaviors, not by using labels.*

  Labels are both shortsighted and not helpful. The label "Jennifer's not a good team player" should be substituted with the statement that says: "Jennifer needs to focus on helping others more during our busy times." The statement "Adam's always late" should become "On Monday and Tuesday, Adam came in 20 minutes past our start time." By shifting the statement away from a negative descriptor and more toward behavior-based actions, you can help the person or the group to understand how and why they need to make changes.

• *Give quick, direct, non-attacking feedback.*

Use specific language. In a group conflict, it's common for the trainer to hear Mary say, "I hate it when Dave leaves my work area a mess," when Dave is also in the room! The trainer's response should be, "Mary, Dave's right here. Turn to him and tell him what you just told me. We're all adults. We should be able to give each other direct, immediate feedback without hurting each other's feelings."

From the supervisor's perspective, the underlying theme of this approach should be, "Don't run to me with every little problem that you should be solving among yourselves. If you have a performance issue with a co-worker, do what you can to solve it right when you see it and not wait days or weeks for me to intervene. If you can't solve it together, using our communication tools, then bring it to me for help."

Feedback can be positive and helpful too. In his best-seller, *The One-Minute Manager*, management guru Ken Blanchard writes of "catching people doing things right," giving them positive strokes right on the spot. "Jerry, I really like it when you . . . "or "Thanks, Marie. It really helps me out when you're able to. . . ."

No one will ever admit that he or she receives *too much praise* from bosses or colleagues. Be direct, on the spot, and stop waiting for the other person to guess what you want or mean.

Some people relish the hurtful power of their words by being bombastic and refusing to see or describe the world in gray areas instead of right-wrong, yes-no, or black-white.

THE LIST OF SEVEN CHOICES

This collection of empowering choices comes from Ms. Jeanne McGuire, one of the principals from McGuire-Pratson Consulting, with offices in Boston and San Diego. Whenever she mediates groups in crisis, she reminds them they all have choices—and not just one or two. Says Ms. McGuire, "Too many people think that they have little or no control over what might happen. I tell them they *always* have options and it's up to them, not others, to decide what to do."

Here are her recommendations to people facing a dilemma as to what to do in a situation where the answers aren't clear:

1. *Leave the situation or the person.*

   This could apply to everything from a bad job to a bad relationship.

2. *Live with the situation or the person.*

   Here, the strategy is to simply find ways to cope.

3. *Change the situation or the person.*

   Tough but possible, this approach requires you to give the person options or choices and to make decisions about the situation that will give you better outcomes.

4. *Change your perception of the situation or the person.*

   Perhaps it just might be you? Seeing things from the other person's perspective may give you some insight into him or her, or at least more self-awareness.

5. *Change your behaviors around the situation or the person.*

   Be different the next time around! As the old saying goes (and there's a good reason some sayings have been around a while): "If you do what you've always done, you'll get what you've always got."

6. *Change both your perceptions and your behaviors.*

   This is certainly the most difficult as well as the most productive. Ask and answer the question, "What do I need to do to be different in this situation?" Cut the other person some slack and come back with a different approach or a different view.

7. *Pretend you've changed.*

   "Here," says Jeanne McGuire with a grin, "you simply have to 'fake it until you make it.'" Meaning, she suggests, smile politely and go along with the person or the situation until you can leave, make changes, or get what you want. This may take days or even years, but it can be a good "secret" strategy if none of the previous six seem palatable.

Some conflict in life and at work is inevitable and unavoidable. But like all other work problems that affect people's performance and productivity, it can and should be managed.

SAMPLE TRAINING PROGRAM SLIDES: THE ESSENTIAL ELEVEN

Use these slides to craft the core of your program, adding or deleting as necessary.

(I'm grateful to Ms. Jeanne McGuire for the use of her slides and training design here. She has substantial experience working with teams in conflict. Her program has been battle-tested and proven to be successful, both in lowering the emotional temperature in the room and in getting results from a once-conflicted team.)

Team and Training Meeting Effectiveness

Goals (what):

Transfer these steps and new tools
to help teams under stress.

Roles (who):

HR Professionals and/or a Facilitator

Process (how):

Ask questions of the group.

Share best practices, give the group tools
for now and resources for later.

What Teams Need

1. Clear Team Purposes and Expectations

2. A Complementary Mix of Skills

3. Concise, Honest, Open Communications

4. A Well-Defined Performance Plan

5. Clearly Defined Roles

6. A Sense of Urgency

7. A Real Sense of Identity and Accountability

Symptoms of Team Stress

- Loss of energy, enthusiasm, momentum
- Loss of focus, purpose
- Unconstructive meetings
- No candor
- People complain, but not to each other
- Heightened conflict
- Cynicism
- Mistrust
- In-fighting
- Excessive blaming, finger-pointing
- Fear, anxiety
- Poor or little results

No one wants to talk about what's really going on!

Six Steps You Can Take

1. Meet briefly with the team.

2. Conduct individual interviews.

3. Facilitate the initial team meeting(s) using new tools.

4. Hold the team accountable to agreements.

5. Facilitate a final team meeting.

6. Install the team tools.

Step 1: Meet Briefly with the Team

- Set the Stage.

  Permission: The highest performing teams successfully deal with conflict.

  Responsibility: Every problem that the team has is a team problem.

- Clarify Goals, Roles, and Processes.

- Get the Team's History.

  Facilitate a discussion on the changes the team has experienced.

Step 2: Conduct Individual Interviews

- Learn the Individual Perceptions.

  Let them blow off steam.

  Help to clarify the crucial issues.

- Consider Using a Self-Assessment Tool or Profile Instrument.

  Understand each person's personal needs and motivations.

  Be prepared to teach them to deal with their differences.

Step 3: Facilitate Team Meeting(s)

- Emphasize the Use of New Tools.
- Get the Team Working on Team Tasks.

Discuss team success requirements.

Initiate the ground rules.

Discuss the results of their
self-assessments/behavioral profiles.

Step 3 (continued)

- Team Requirements Tool:

  Roles and expertise

  Challenges the team is facing

  Outcomes from our facilitated sessions

- Ground Rules Tool:

  Attitudes and behaviors the team values
  and agrees to demonstrate

- The Tools:

  Listening, questioning, expressing

  Giving and receiving feedback

  Conflict management

  Problem solving

Step 4: Hold Team Accountable to Agreements

- Allow four weeks to integrate the new tools, goals, decisions, and accomplishments.

- Learn and appreciate small successes.

Step 5: Facilitate Final Team Meeting

- Identify current successes since the last session.

- Continue to problem solve and teach the team to continue to use its tools.

- Create team and individual action plans.

Step 6: Install the Team Tools

- Stay in touch and reconvene in six months.

- Assure gains are sustained:

    Perceptual breakthroughs

    Behavioral breakthroughs

- Part of the team's promise is to stay focused and on track.

10

Teaching a Realistic Stress Management Program

Brain cells create ideas.
Stress kills brain cells. Stress is not a good idea.

—Frederick Saunders

Key

The title to this chapter is intentional. If people are going to give you their time to help them manage something as serious, personal, and potentially life-threatening (if left unmanaged) as their own stress levels, you had better supply realistic, practical, and worthwhile tools. This is not a program that's designed to eliminate stress; that's neither possible nor realistic. It's a training intervention that gives people proven and reliable coping skills to help them deal with an issue that they may be in denial that they even have.

Plenty of people who lived a hard-and-fast life only made changes after a significant threat to their mental and physical health. Your job is to help the participants—no matter where they see themselves on a personal stress measurement, ranging from "I'm fine" to "I'm falling apart."

Usual Audience

Truth be told, this program tends to "sell" best to HR as a "reward" for the workforce. I usually position it as a "wellness program" to HR, since they're often looking for ways to provide various low-cost, high-impact perks to the employees. You can do this program over a lunch hour, as a mandatory session for all hands; as part of a brown bag session for those who want to eat and relax; or as part of a half-day session for all or interested employees.

I tend to see a large number of frontline employees in these sessions, and it's no secret why. Any worker who has a high human contact/low control job is a candidate for a stress management program. You're bound to see a room full of employees who deal with angry customers, cranky taxpayers, unpaid vendors, and other internal or external life-drainers.

Best Length

I've taught this program in as little as an hour (with my foot on the content gas pedal the whole time) and as long as eight hours. It tends to work best in the two- to four-hour range, especially if the participants can end by going to lunch or going home. You'll need at least 20 minutes at the end to conduct the relaxation exercise—a vital part of the program and a piece that you should not skip.

Basic Training Themes

I actually enjoy teaching stress management programs because I feel the expectations are a bit less from the participants. They sort of know what they expect to hear, but they don't have a lot of preconceptions or misconceptions coming in. For a program with voluntary attendance, I always start by saying, "Thank you for coming. Those of you who are here probably don't need this training as much as those who didn't come."

For the most part, you're going to have a fairly open-minded audience, with fewer of the tough participants we saw in Chapters Two and Three. As such, a stress management course should feature a design that's easy for you to teach and easier for them to absorb. The ingredients for this are three: fun, easy, and filled with facts. Here's a sample agenda.

Here's What Stress Is. A fact of life; something we all have to cope with; an issue that affects different people in different ways; and an issue that not only impacts your personal and professional life, but has a powerful mind-body connection as well.

Here's What Stress Can Do to Your Mind and Body. The connection between stress and disease is clear; the negative effects on your heart, weight, and physical and mental health have been well-established. Either you manage it throughout your life, or you may pay a painful price at some point.

Here Are Some Coping Tools. Make better choices; manage your time more carefully; don't commit to things you really don't want to do; stay connected with good people and avoid toxic personalities or situations; take vacations; live more in the moment and enjoy what is around you; learn self-relaxation techniques; exercise enough to earn your shower; try to eat more carefully; and develop ways to improve the quality and quantity of sleep.

Here Is a Focused Relaxation Exercise You Can Do Yourself, to Manage Your Own Stress, Whenever You Need To. Find a safe, comfortable place; sit upright in a comfortable chair (where you're less likely to fall asleep); listen to some soft, no-words music; close your eyes and relax your whole body, part by part, from head to foot. Spend 20 minutes per day in this endeavor, breathing slowly and not thinking about anything, and you'll add years to your life.

Current Organizational Policies

While there are not usually any company policies that address stress as a business reality (and perhaps there should be), this issue does have a connection to the company Employee Assistance Program (EAP). Teaching this material offers a platinum opportunity to remind all attendees about the existence of the EAP (assuming the organization has an EAP provider, of course). People don't necessarily think of their EAP as a resource during stressful periods, although they should.

It makes sense to discuss the EAP relationship because it's usually fraught with myths. While I firmly believe EAPs can save lives and rescue careers, people don't go for three reasons: they don't know the EAP exists; they don't believe it's confidential; and they don't believe they either need help or can be helped. I spend as much time as I can discussing the EAP contact numbers, the absolute confidentiality of their work, and the myriad of stress-reducing issues they cover, including financial problems; marital strife; gambling, drug, and/or alcohol addictions; depression and other mental illnesses; coping with sick children or parents; adoptions; and blended step-families.

"The first call is usually the hardest to make," I tell the group, "and the first appointment is usually the hardest to go to, but once you do go, you'll wonder why it took you so long to make the right decision."

The Organizational Culture and Climate

There are usually two reasons why you'll be called on to present stress-management-related material: As usual, the need may have been driven by an event, or the HR department is forward-thinking and progressive enough to see it as a wellness issue. In the first case, senior management, often working in concert with HR, has seen a sharp rise in customer or vendor complaints, accidents or injuries, overtime, absenteeism, anonymous or vocal complaints, employee dissatisfaction with customers or supervisors, and supervisor dissatisfaction with employees. In other words, people aren't getting along and the strife is starting to cost the company money.

In the second possibility, the HR department, which fields many of the calls related to the above-mentioned complaints, sees a stress management program as a gift to give the employees. They also may be wise enough to forecast that a little training on this subject now may minimize the workers' compensation claims down the road.

The (Real) Purpose of the Program

Like other tough training topics, whose benefit is not always obvious and whose value is hard to measure, stress management programs can be seen by one sector in senior management as a feel-good, do-nothing waste of time and resources. For other executives, in and out of HR—and this is a jaded perspective to be sure—the installation of a regular stress management training program (biannually, once per quarter, twice during the busy holiday season) can be a way to assuage their guilt for not doing much to support the employees during other times of the year.

Like providing outplacement services for employees caught in a mass layoff (which often has no "real" economic value to the company save for easing their collective guilty minds), stress programs can give some executives an excuse to say or imply to the employees, "See what we gave to you to help you cope? Now get back to work!"

Their Learning Keys

Besides learning the fine points about the R.E.D.S. mnemonic for stress management (as mentioned in the slide samples: Relaxation, Exercise, Diet, Sleep), it's important that you demonstrate the 20-minute focused relaxation exercise. Follow the description in the next section and re-review the Future Pacing discussion located in Chapter Two.

Your Teaching Keys

Always, always start by focusing on the positive. This course *should* be relaxing, fun, and filled with quick and easy tools people can learn, use, and remember later on. I always say the same thing, "This is a program just for you. I'll do all of the work. You only have to listen to me. If you want to take notes, that's fine. And if you don't want to take notes, that's fine too. Coming to a stress management workshop shouldn't be a stressful experience."

One way to help your group remember the key tools for better stress management is the R.E.D.S. mnemonic: Relaxation, Exercise, Diet, and Sleep.

Relaxation. Increase the amount of time spent in quiet activities such as reading, relaxing, and engaging in hobbies and other pleasurable activities. Many people have found ancient yet non-traditional forms of relaxation like yoga, tai chi, controlled breathing, self-hypnosis, and meditation to offer many benefits and help for a stressful life.

Exercise. Exercise is an extremely effective method for counteracting the effects of stress. Studies suggest 30 minutes per day, three to five times per week seems to give the best stress-relieving results. Always check with your doctor before starting any exercise program.

Diet. Try to eliminate foods or beverages heavy in sugar, caffeine, fat, and alcohol, all of which can help to trigger stress responses in the body. Although these ingredients may be found in some of our favorite "feel good" foods or drinks, too much of any of them can make your body feel worse. Try to start your day with healthy protein, not sugar-laden carbohydrates.

Sleep. Most adults are chronically sleep-deprived, often getting by on way less than the recommended eight hours. Develop pre-sleep rituals (showering; reading; low-key, peaceful activities) and make your bedroom dark, quiet, and cool.

Besides the material you cover in the sample agenda, you'll want to teach the group about brain wave activity, because this foreshadows the work you will do in the focused relaxation exercise.

In essence, there are four levels of brain wave activity: the Beta, Alpha, Theta, and Delta levels. Here's a brief, non-medical description of what happens to you when you're in each level. Although the brain wave activity levels are shown in order of fastest to slowest, I'll save the discussion of the Alpha level for last, since it's the most important for our relaxation exercise:

Beta. Wide awake, alert, and fully conscious. This is our normal activity level throughout our day.

Alpha. The relaxation state.

Theta. This level occurs when you are in REM or rapid eye movement sleep. REM sleep is characterized by the brief twitching of your eyes when you sleep, signifying a dreaming state.

Delta. Dead asleep here, with no REM or dream activity. This is you sleeping at your heaviest.

So if Delta is a heavy sleep stage, and Theta is REM or dream sleep, and Beta is a wide-awake stage, what happens in the Alpha state? In Alpha, you're half-awake and half-asleep. You can hear others in the room or certain sounds, but you don't care. If you've ever been alone on a long car ride, on a rainy day, where it's warm inside and soft radio music is playing, and you're watching the windshield wipers go back and forth, back and forth, back and forth, you've been in the Alpha state. Why? Because at one point in this peaceful reverie, you either almost drove off the road, missed your exit completely, or drifted into another lane and were brought back to the Beta state by the sound of an approaching car horn.

Alpha is a peaceful, restful, not asleep-not awake state where your mind and body can relax, rejuvenate, and recuperate. More important, the Alpha state is where your unconscious mind (or subconscious mind) gets a break from the demands put on it by your conscious mind. In other words, the Alpha state is where meditation, guided hypnosis, self-hypnosis, and focused relaxation can take place.

For stress management to work, the more often people can put themselves into the Alpha state, the better they will feel. Keep in mind that this stage is not sleep; it's half-sleep, but it's also half-attention, meaning people can hear and interpret their own thoughts, commands, or instructions (self-hypnosis), or the words, commands, or instructions of a facilitator (hypnosis). Remind the group that no one will ever do anything in the Alpha state that he or she wouldn't do while fully awake. "Therefore," I tell my groups, "if you want to cluck like a chicken during the relaxation exercise, that's your choice, not mine!"

So here is one way to run the focused relaxation exercise, which you should build into your training design for the last 30 minutes of your session:

1. It's best to start this after the group has had one last biology break. When they're on break, put up a slide with a peaceful landscape photo, or a fractal (get an inviting one off the Internet). Invite them to sit as comfortably as possible in their chairs, feet flat on the floor, hands in their lap, cell phones off.

2. Start playing your CD music and, using *your lapel microphone now,* invite them to listen for a few moments. (The music should be peaceful, pleasant, lyric-free, and low-key. Be sure to play music

you have permission to use.) Move to the *back of the room* as you ask this and get close to the room light switches.

3. Ask the group to focus on their own favorite parts of the photo for a few moments. Tell them you will count from 1 to 5 as they stare at the photo, and at 5, you will ask them to close their eyes comfortably and easily. Count from 1 to 5 and at 5, turn off all of the room lights.

4. As the music plays, invite them to get comfortable and keep their eyes closed. Begin a guided "body relaxation tour" for them, starting at the top of their heads and going down to their toes. Talk them through a slow and easy process to relax each body area. (I use this as my constant mantra: "heavy, warm, safe, and relaxed, drifting down, drifting down, drifting down.").

5. Once you've helped them to relax their whole bodies, tell them that you will soon ask them to begin counting from 100 down to 1, by ones. Repeat this again and then ask them to begin counting down.*

6. Repeat these two deepening phrases from time to time: "Some of you may hear the sound of my voice as I talk, and some of you may not. And that's perfectly fine. Some of you may hear sounds, inside or outside the room, and these will simply help you relax even more deeply."

7. Go back and remind the group to keep counting down, from 100 down to 1, by ones, and if they lose their place, to simply start where they remember leaving off. Suggest if they reach the number 1, they can simply start over again, counting down from 100. (Few people can keep track of the counting to get all the way down to the number 1; the session is just too relaxing to have to focus that hard.)

---

*My thanks to Mr. Bob Otto, master hypnotist—at www.robertottohypnosis.com—for teaching me his "confusion technique," as seen in Steps 5 through 8.

8. Alternate between Steps 6 and 7 for about 10 minutes.

9. Tell them how peaceful they feel and how they can get to this place of peace any time they want to, simply by touching their thumb and first finger together, on either hand, and hearing themselves say the word "Pax" (Latin for "peace"). This is called "setting an anchor" and you will want to repeat it for them about five to seven times.

10. Take them back to full alertness and full attention by asking them to feel energy coming back to their bodies, starting at their toes and moving up to their heads. Count as you help them visualize this energy, from 5 to 1, asking them to come to full awake when they hear the number 1. (I usually snap my fingers for emphasis at "one" and click the lights back on at the same moment.)

This whole relaxation exercise should take you about 20 to 25 minutes. If you've done it correctly and used the tools—the music; the photo; the lapel mike; a nice, easy, and slightly robotic monotone (the same pace and volume you would use to lull a child to sleep with a bedtime story); the counting technique (which distracts the conscious mind enough for you to reach the subconscious or unconscious mind with the thumb-finger and "Pax" anchors); and the implanted idea that they can replicate this relaxation process any time they need to—you will win rave reviews, even from the skeptics who told you or others "they couldn't relax" at the beginning of the program.

Your Success Tools

PowerPoint™ slides, some exercises, a brief handout package for the group (less is more), and some pleasant screenshots/photos (seascapes, meadows, country scenes, snow, sunsets, fractals, or other peaceful scenes) that you can show as focus points for the start of the relaxation exercise. (Some trainers like to download a copy of an older stress measurement tool from the Internet. Known as the Holmes-Rahe Scale, it's a bit dated but still works as a useful handout.)

For the focused relaxation exercise, you'll need a CD of appropriate, New Age–type relaxation music, a good CD player (use your laptop CD player only as a last resort because the small speakers tend to mute the quality of the music), external music speakers for the CD player (if you can get them), and the most important tool, a lapel microphone.

The lapel microphone is crucial to conduct the exercise. Beg, borrow, or steal one if you must, because the amplification of your voice, coupled with the relaxing, non-competitive music, helps the group to relax at a deeper level. The use of the microphone changes their perspective because they think it's one of the tools of your trade. Even if you didn't use the microphone for any other part of the presentation, strap it on for this part. It helps them make the leap to participate in the exercise, by adding a bit of drama to the proceedings.

Potholes and Sandpits

This program is not about you giving people amateur psychotherapy, medical advice, or relationship tips. You may be asked questions related to these issues, either publicly or when a person comes to you during a break or after the session asking for advice. Some people are looking for permission to make changes in their lives and they want you to give it to them. Resist their efforts to put you in control of their lives or decisions.

I had a woman once ask me if she should bring up some of my stress management techniques to her support group, which focused on parents who had lost a child to cancer. I tried to be as supportive and general as I could, saying, "I know your group leader probably has some tips of his or her own. Why don't you bring it up with him or her privately, before the next group session?"

You may be faced with these types of questions: "I'm having stress in my marriage. Should I leave my husband or wife?" or "My job causes me stress. Do you think I should quit?" I always try to ask reflexive questions back to them, for example, "I'm just a trainer. Have you considered talking to a licensed professional about these concerns? Have you contacted your organization's EAP provider for a referral?"

I make a number of references to taking more of a "Zen approach" to life, that is, to try and live "in the moment" and enjoy what you are doing, while you are doing it. Whether it's simply enjoying a sip of good coffee, a nice song on the car radio, or the breeze on your face as you walk from the car to the office, living in the moment makes the world more bearable. For some reason, during one program, several highly religious people took great offense to this and complained bitterly to the HR manager who had brought me in. They believed my remarks went against God and Jesus. They believed that my asking the group to consider a Zen lifestyle was the same as asking them to discount or give up their own religious beliefs.

I believe these people were overly zealous and knew nothing about Zen, which accepts all religious beliefs, deities, and faiths as valid. In future sessions with other groups, I gave more of an explanation along these lines and heard no other complaints. If you're not comfortable with the Zen piece, drop it from your discussion points.

Some Fine Points

For me and many of the participants who have been through my version of stress management, the focused relaxation is the highlight of the program. If you're going to do it, do it right. Go to the bookstore and get some good books on meditation, self-hypnosis, and relaxation. (The *Dummies* books and the *Complete Idiots Guides* are a good place to start.)

Next, buy some high-quality CDs featuring relaxation-specific music. I use several CDs that feature peaceful, non-competitive, lyric-free music, combined with natural sounds, like water, rainfall, waves, or the wind. Using these CDs in the background as you take the participants through the head-to-toe relaxation process, the guided imagery, and the use of an anchor can bring great results.

Practice on yourself first, using the CDs and some quality headphones, to put yourself in the Alpha state. It's quite habit-forming, and the more you do it, the more you want to do it. You need to feel the same feelings as your audience, so you can replicate the experience for them in the training environment. (For additional guidance in focused relaxation with a specific purpose, go back and re-read the Future Pacing Exercise material in Chapter Two).

SAMPLE TRAINING PROGRAM SLIDES: THE NECESSARY NINE

Use these slides to craft the core of your program, adding or deleting as necessary.

Our Agenda

- What is stress? Is there good stress and bad stress?

- Who or what creates your stress?

- What can stress do to your mind and body?

- How can you best learn to cope with stress?

What Is Stress?

- Do we always have stress in our lives?

- The result of changes or comfort zone shifts?

- Can we have both positive and negative stress?

- Is it related to our hormones?

- Does it affect our thinking?

- Can it affect how we feel?

Stress Symptoms

Behavioral: under- or over-eating, alcohol and drug use, compulsive behavior, anger, rage, violence to self or others

Cognitive: distracted thoughts, concentration problems, can't think clearly, intrusive thoughts, problems sleeping, making more mistakes

Emotional: anxiety, depression, anger, fears, tears

Medical: backaches and headaches, heart attacks, ulcers, immune system problems, fatigue, low energy

Physiological: tense muscles, high blood pressure, rapid pulse, stomach problems

- What do I like about my job?

- What bugs me about my job?

- How can I cope with, manage, or get closure on my Bug List items?

The Five Stages of Job Burnout

- Stage 1—The Good Years

- Stage 2—Energy Down/Apathy Up

- Stage 3—The Stress Symptoms Start

- Stage 4—The Clock Ticks

- Stage 5—The Mind/Body Crash

How many of you feel you're in Stage 3 right now?

Stress Management Tools

- Keep to your daily routines.

- Seek support from family, friends, and colleagues.

- Go on a "news diet."

- Only do things, for yourself and others, that give you purpose and satisfaction. Say "no" more.

- Get a pet.

Re-Balance Your Life

- Make your life easier when you can. (Hire people to do the things you hate!)

- Stop saying "I can't believe it" when things go wrong.

- Watch your language and negative self-talk.

- Use the P.I.N. technique for new ideas. (Positive first, then Interesting, then Negative)

- Become a "Zen master" and live in the moment you are in right now. Enjoy the little things.

Take the "R.E.D.S." Stress "Cure"

Relax Your Body: Relax for 20 minutes, once or twice per day.

Exercise: Try for at least 30 minutes, three to five times per week.

Diet: Go easy on fats, sugar, alcohol, and caffeine.

Sleep: Develop pre-sleep rituals, such as showering or reading.

Good Relationships: Stay connected with positive people.

Find Life Beyond Work: Get back to your old hobbies, other friends outside of work.

Set Boundaries: Know how to say "no" to things you don't really want to do.

Got Stress? Got 20 Minutes?

Use Self-Hypnosis, Meditation, or Relaxation

1. Slow and Steady Breathing

2. Use Head-to-Toe Muscle Relaxation

3. Create Peaceful Imagery in Your Mind

11

Tips from the
Training Trenches
Some Finer Points

It's not how smart you are; it's how smart you can make them.

—Lessons from Chairman Karl (Albrecht)

Key

This chapter provides a capstone to our efforts. Like the first chapter, it puts some unique touches on the training experience so that you can teach tough topics, confident that you have done all you can do to succeed. It also seeks to give your confidence one last boost, knowing that you can go out and teach tough training topics to any audience.

Dealing with Repetition: Keeping It Fresh Time After Time After Time

If you've been to a real New York Broadway play, it's easy to marvel at the skills of the actors and actresses, giving their all, night after night. Musing over coffee or drinks after the performance, you say to yourself or your friends, "How do they do it? How do they keep that energy, two hours per night, show after show, for weeks, or even months? Don't they get bored? Don't they get tired? Don't they ever feel like just going through the motions, and mailing it in once in a while?"

The answers to these questions, in order, are: "They're professionals. They know that most of the people in the audience have never seen the performance, so it's new for them." "Yes, but they're pros, so they work hard and submerge their boredom." "Yes, but they're pros, so they run on adrenaline until the curtain falls." "Sure, but they don't, because they are pros and pros don't give half of a performance."

And so it goes with training programs that you are asked (or required) to give over and over, on the same subject(s), to one fresh group after the other. It's tough, but you do your job and you go home or back to the hotel and get ready to do it again tomorrow, just like the star of the Broadway play, who has to carry the whole show, or all the way down to the twelfth chorus member in the back, who is seen but not heard.

Recently, I was called on by a client to teach a series of one-hour seminars, with half of the program to cover a new workplace violence policy and the other half to cover an existing drug and alcohol use policy.

"Great!" I said, "How many sessions?"

"Fourteen," said the HR director.

"Not all at once, right? We're going to spread them out a bit, right?" I said, gulping silently.

"Sure," said the HR director, "Five on one day, six on the second day, and three on the third day."

"Three days in a row?" I asked, starting to imagine my fate: hunched over the podium, clutching my ever-hoarsening throat, and trying to calculate if I was teaching Session 4 or Session 11.

"See you next week," said the HR director, cheerily.

So I did it, teaching fourteen sessions over three days, covering the same eight slides every time, in the same order. I trained six hundred people in one-hour increments, with 15 minutes between sessions. At the end, I was nothing but a puddle and some teeth.

They were kind enough to give me a 90-minute lunch break each day, which allowed me to eat and, on the final day, take a 20-minute recovery nap in my car.

I taught each session the same way, with variations in the order of my accompanying stories and well-polished jokes. I used the energy of the crowds (sometimes as many as ninety people at a time, down to eight people for one session, the CEO and his staff) to help pull me through. I engaged in as much Q and A as I could in the limited time. And since the subject matter for each topic can be fraught with complexities (for example, "Are they allowed to search my locker for drugs or a gun?"), I was on my toes throughout.

To her credit, the HR director opened every session and had at least one member of her support staff attend every session. Her support staff also replenished the handouts, pens, food, drinks, and feedback sheets. This made it easy for me to sit like a statue in between each program.

What kept me going through this trudge was the fact that another outside trainer (a longtime colleague of mine) would follow in my footstomps with an even tougher gig: fourteen one-hour sessions on the company's sexual harassment policy refresher. At least I had the "luxury" of having two topics to go back and forth with; my pal went through the same three-day schedule on one issue, alone. He survived, and so did I.

There are two important things to keep in mind about teaching the same program with mind- (and foot-) numbing repetition. First, the people who brought you in (either an internal or an external client) don't care about your issues. They're probably nice folks, but they don't care about your tired feet, your sinus headache, or the stirrings of your sore throat. They don't care that you're tired of telling the same stories, reciting the same policies, or showing the same slides. They're paying you for your results, whether you work as an employee or as an outside consultant. As such, you're expected to be a pro, just like the Broadway actor or actress.

Second, the audience doesn't know or care that this is the twenty-third time you've taught this program. If they haven't seen it before, it's new to them. You would think that whining to the participants about the number of times you've had to teach the material would earn you some bonus points. It does you absolutely no good to complain about being tired or bored. At a minimum, it comes across as irritating. At a maximum, it's simply unprofessional.

Keep in mind that many people see trainers as extroverted, popular, and knowledgeable; otherwise, how would "they" have put you up there to teach everyone? No matter what, stay in your role as a professional facilitator. Gripe to your trainer-colleagues later, not to your audience, ever. (Many people also see training and speaking as a highly compensated activity, which it is and it isn't, depending. As such, griping about what some see as a well-paid job is like the pro sports athlete complaining that the hot tub is broken in his hotel suite.)

If you want to get good feedback, you'll *appear* just as fresh for the last session as you did for the first. Be tired on the inside, save your energy when you can, pound the go juice (coffee) and fat pills (glazed doughnuts) if you must, but have the stamina necessary to complete your task.

The Stopwatch: A Trainer's Best Friend

One of the best training tools I have came from the Internet. Because I seemed to have more and more problems getting people back from breaks, lunches, and exercises, I purchased a software program featuring a stopwatch. Time kept getting away from everyone, and besides stressing me, it's not good for the pace or flow of the session. Since it's no fun to have to crack the whip and beg/plead to get people back in their seats and to get their full attention, I've let technology take over.

I have a simple digital stopwatch program on my training laptop computer. I can pull it up whenever I need it, set the time to elapse backwards down to zero, and then ring a fairly pleasant alarm bell when time is up. Because this stopwatch can be embedded into the PowerPoint™ slides, you can see the large numbers from any part of the room.

I tell the group that I will set the timer for whatever break, lunch, or exercise period we need (10, 15, 60 minutes, or any number) and tell them that we will resume again as soon as the time runs out. I remind them to check the screen occasionally and monitor their return or their outputs to finish up and get back and into their seats just before the stopwatch clicks down to zero.

Go to the Internet and enter "stopwatch software" into your search engine of choice. Test a few of the programs to get one that fits your laptop and features numbers large enough to be seen from a good distance in the training room.

When it comes to managing their time, most adults hate being told what to do. The beauty of the stopwatch visual is that it helps you out by keeping them on task and on time, without you having to nag them constantly to return to their seats.

The Comic's Tool Kit: Don't Forget to Leave Some Jokes at Home

There is nothing worse than when you tell a joke in a public forum and it falls flat. Whether the joke was great and the group was bad or both were bad or you just didn't tell it right, there are few "sounds" on earth worse than uncomfortable silence.

I stand corrected; the only thing worse than a joke, witty remark, or a sly aside that falls flat is the trainer who compounds the error by repeating it or embarrassing the group because they didn't get it. As any good standup comic will tell you, move on as if it never happened. Let it go and get back to your business.

As comic legend George Carlin suggests, "Humor really is life and death. When you're going great, it's 'I was *killing* them out there!' and if you're going bad, it's 'I was *dying* out there.'"

Using humor in training programs has many risks, which is why I absolutely avoid telling any kind of topical, political, religious, or alternative lifestyle jokes. My stuff tends to be very self-deprecating; for example, when I stumble over my words or flub a remark, I say, "This is why I can't buy my teeth through the mail; I have to go right to the dentist" or "This is why I can't drink tequila for breakfast."

I don't use the training platform as a way to tell old saws, like: "A guy walks into a bar . . ." or "A guy says to his wife. . . ." This isn't Open Mike Night down at the coffeehouse; it's a professional environment, where humor should be used as a spice, not as a main course.

The two rules of thumb for using humor during training programs are simple and unbreakable: (1) Don't pick on any one person in the crowd and (2) don't laugh, in a phony way, at your own jokes.

Let's take the first one. I've certainly teased some people in the group, only over small things, and only after I've built plenty of rapport with them. You can get away with chiding someone in a gentle way. It can create closeness with the crowd and humanize you, especially if you connect your own foibles to theirs.

An example: In my workplace violence program, I use the name "Crazy Larry" as sort of a stock character, whenever I need to give an example of a certain type of inappropriate behavior. (As I noted in the opening quote for Chapter Six, this is related to Larry Hansel, a mentally ill former employee who shot and killed two executives at a San Diego firm where he had worked.) I always ask, in a smiling way, if there actually is anybody named Larry in the group and it gets a bit of a laugh if not, and a huge one if there is, because everybody turns to look at their Larry, to see his reaction. I always follow up by going over to their Larry, shaking his hand, and bantering a bit about how I'm not really referring to him, "but if the shoe fits . . . " or "Cover me! I'm going for coffee!" or something similar.

Since I start by telling them I will use more humor than they expect in this program, I have a bit of a free pass when it comes to this point. (As I mentioned in Chapter Six on workplace violence, this subject demands that you not scare the participants with blood-and-guts tales from the media.) I've already told them I'm going to try to make an uncomfortable subject less frightening, so they're more on the lookout for examples of a lighter touch throughout.

To put more of an edge on this issue, I'm very careful never to insult any member of the audience, especially any of the senior executives, who have either brought me in or are there watching my performance. The real truth of training is that senior people often attend the programs (that they mandate their employees to go to), not because they plan on learning anything new, but more as a token gesture. I have witnessed many examples where the senior executive introduces me by saying "how important this subject is and how it's very important for us all to pay careful attention" and then leaves for good as soon as I start talking.

I've seen many others leave at the first break, convinced that they "know enough now" or have shown their faces sufficiently to the rest of the employees. Don't think this goes unnoticed on the feedback sheets: "I see my boss skipped out early" or "I noticed there were no managers in the room after the break."

Trainers who like to start off by making the senior-most person in the room the butt of some stupid joke risk alienating that person (which is bad for their future economic health) or, just as bad, alienating the group at large, who may be quite fond of that person. Don Rickles can get away with this approach; the rest of us can't and shouldn't try it.

The second caveat—laughing at your own material—breaks the cardinal rule of professional comedians. They *know* the joke is funny; that's why they told it. They don't need to laugh; that's what the crowd is for. Mimic this style: If you have a great and funny story or better joke, tell it and let it make its own laughs.

Landing the Helicopter: More Slides Than Time

If you train like I do, and fall in love with the sound of your own voice like I do from time to time, it's easy to run out of program before you run out of slides, handouts, policies, or similar "must cover" materials. Sometimes you make a nice connection with the group and they lead you into tangential discussions that can be fruitful, albeit time-consuming. Other times, you can find that one question from the participants leads to another, and so on, until the minutes have quickly slipped away. Last, you can find yourself behind when the group comes back late from breaks or lunches, or from exercises you've given them. (Go back and re-read the Stopwatch Software section above again.)

Any way you find yourself behind, it can be chilling to realize that you have to cover a significant amount of material in a very short period of time. This begs a larger question: Do you *have* to cover every slide in the packet of handout materials? The short answer is: It depends.

It depends on whether you have included the slide as part of the handout. If so, you have to cover it, even in passing. If you skip the slide completely, it may not bother some of the participants, but it will irritate many of them. And for those people who need closure when it comes to processing information, it will really annoy them.

If the slide is not part of the handouts, then you can omit it from your discussion, unless, of course, it is germane to the reason you're there (policy points, new guidelines, safety issues, and so on). If it absolutely must be included, then include it. If not, take a tip from master trainer Bob Pike (Creative Training Techniques) and use his categories to decide whether you share it with the audience:

- *Need to Know*—This information must be covered. Make cuts to the materials somewhere else.

- *Nice to Know*—This information is interesting but not critical, urgent, or required. Cover it if you have the time.

- *Where to Find It*—Simply remind the audience where they can find this type of information (off their intranet/office network, in the back or in an appendix attachment to their handouts, in their policy manual, and so on).

As a solution to the "too much material/too little time" dilemma, perhaps it helps to consider the metaphor of the helicopter. As an instrument to cover ground, the helicopter is a powerful tool in aviation. It can fly high, looking over a huge expanse of area, or it can hover a few feet off the ground or even land quickly when necessary.

In the training environment, the helicopter offers a useful symbol, with you at the pilot controls. You can give a broad overview at a more strategic level (sky high) or you can bring the chopper down to an operational level (ground it), simply by changing your focus or tone, on the fly, as it were.

When time is against you, it's probably best to push the stick forward and get your craft onto the ground as fast as possible.

The Easel Process: Write Exactly What They Say

The scene is a familiar one. You, as the presenter, are asking the group for some help on a particular problem or issue. Example:

You:	"So what's another way we can cut costs in the plant for the third quarter?"
Participant 1:	"How about reviewing our long-distance phone bills for errors?"
You write:	"Look at utility bills."
You:	"What else have we come up with?"
Participant 2:	"How about we look at our electrical and water usage rates?"
You write:	A check mark next to "Look at utility bills," as in, "It's up there already."

So in a few short strokes of the pen, you've totally alienated Participant 1 and Participant 2 by violating a cardinal rule of recording brainstorming ideas: *Don't edit their words without their express permission.*

For the rest of the session (and perhaps others in the future), these folks will look at what you have crafted and say to themselves, "That's not what I said. The facilitator wrote what he or she *thought* I said, not what I actually said. Those are not my words up there on that easel pad. I'm checking out."

Don't paraphrase for the sake of expediency or space. Write exactly what they say, as they say it, for example, "Review our long-distance phone bills for errors" and "Look at our electrical and water usage rates."

If you have needs about space or time, get their permission to shorten what they have said. Draw it out of them by putting a fence around their words, until you have a summarizing answer that satisfies them. Only when you have the person's approval should you move forward; for example, "Dave, did I capture what you said correctly, without putting words in your mouth?" or "Mary, can you give me a bit more concise version of what you just said? I don't want to lose your idea. I just want you to help me get it into a written form that's right for both of us."

The Review Pledge

In our information-driven society, the knowledge you're attempting to impart is competing constantly with every other factoid that's bombarding your audience. Whether they're getting overloaded at home, at work, or via every media source (including junk mail, e-mail, and ads in elevators) that exists currently, it's hard to get what you say to stick, regardless of how good it is or you are. As one cynical old newspaper editor once said, "Let's face it, these days even the Second Coming of Christ will only get about 1,500 words above the fold."

One of the ways I try to combat this in-one-ear-and-out-the-other syndrome is to get the participants to take The Pledge. In a good-natured and humorous way, I usually wait until we've come back from the first break to say, "Please raise your right hands and repeat after me: I promise—Louder please!—I promise (a few reply) to look at this material again (most reply), in about a week (by now they almost always all reply and then they all laugh)."

I remind them that about 50 percent of what we talk about or what I teach them may leave their heads as soon as they leave the training room. (Perhaps this is being too generous with some audiences I've had, where I can tell by their faces that 75 percent or more of what I just said has floated out of their skulls, never to return.)

So in about one week, they should sit down with the handout materials and a cup of coffee, and "take" the seminar again in their heads, looking at the slides, their notes, and any other attached material. This approach provides a good-natured way to remind the group of an important issue: "I can only lead you to the water; I cannot make you drink it. It's up to you to shoulder the retention responsibility after this session ends. I've just given you an easy and painless way to recall much of what we discussed here, at a time and place that works best for you."

Working the Feedback Sheets

My main beef with feedback sheets is my main complaint with performance evaluations: There is no standardized form. Different organizations measure the training experience in different ways, some fairly effectively and others so poorly that it actually hurts the training process (and the trainer's ego) to gather the information.

For example, one large training organization uses a statement on its evaluation form that reads, "Comparing all my previous experiences, this was the best." Compared to what? Meeting the Pope? Landing on the moon? The birth of your child?

In some examples I've seen, the feedback statements are far too general, offering the participants a fast and limited way out: Just check some boxes or circle some numbers on a 1 to 10 scale and you're done. In other examples, the sheets are far too open-ended, asking vague questions that force the participants to write several paragraphs to provide their feedback. Few people want to write much more than a few sentences, unless they thought the program was great or hideous. Not surprisingly, these essay-type feedback forms aren't filled out too completely, as the attendees beat a hasty retreat for the door.

The best feedback sheets I've seen tend to ask the most pertinent questions:

- The length of the program was: too short, too long, just right.

- The pace of the program was: too slow, too fast, just right.

- Today I learned: more than I expected, about what I expected, less than I expected.

- Rate the instructor's knowledge of the subject: poor, fair, average, above average, excellent.

- Rate the instructor's presentation style: poor, fair, average, above average, excellent.

- How helpful were the handouts: poor, fair, average, above average, excellent.

- How helpful were the program slides: poor, fair, average, above average, excellent.

- What topic or subject did you find most valuable?

- What topic or subject did you find least valuable?

- What changes would you make to this program?

- What was the best skill you learned or the most valuable piece of information for you?

- Any other comments?

Get good examples of ones that work for your style and use them as a template to create your own. Give them to the clients, instead of relying on their (often less than useful) version.

The Scent of the Reward: Why We Do It

I devised this book as a guide for presenters of every stripe: attorneys, new and veteran trainers, one-person training departments, consultants, and the like. Much of the focus of a book on tough training topics has its emphasis on the negative, "Here's how to get through and get along with tough audiences and tough topics."

Yet, as hard as it can be to stand in front of other people and convince them that you know what you're training about, we wouldn't do it if the payoffs weren't rich. As any professional, successful (you can be one and not the other) standup comic will tell you, there are few greater things in life than eliciting hearty and spontaneous laughter from a crowd.

It can be deeply satisfying to know that other people have learned something new, different, or even life-changing or career-changing through your efforts on the training platform. I have had grizzled employees with thirty-plus years or more on the job make a special trip up to where I was standing at the end of the program simply to shake my hand and tell me, "I've been here a long time. This was one of the best training programs I've ever been to. I just wanted to tell you that."

I have read feedback sheets that have said, "This instructor was the most knowledgeable person on this subject that I've ever seen. Sitting through this program was an absolute pleasure and I will make it a point to tell others to come."

There have been times when I've finished up, thanked the group, and begun to pack up my goodies, when I've looked up to see a long line of employees, waiting patiently, just wanting to shake my hand and say thanks. It did and still does warm my heart to think they would take a moment of their day to express their gratitude to a guy just trying to do a good job.

After teaching a class on safety and security to a large group of city librarians, I wrapped it up and thanked them for their participation and attention.

They applauded and I lowered my head in a polite gesture of thanks for their kindness. When I raised my eyes again, what I thought was them clapping as they were leaving turned into a rousing and spontaneous standing ovation, with shouts and cheers to match. As I stood grinning at them and waving like a rock star, it was hard not to burst into tears out of gratitude (and I'm a pretty macho guy). To say I never touched the ground as I walked to my car understates it.

You already know these moments are possible in the training environment. You *can* win them over, even before you ever open your mouth. You *can* win them over, even if they started out hating the topic or thinking they were going to hate the trainer. You *can* win them over to your side, by connecting with them, laughing with them, telling them real and human stories, and by making their understanding of the subject important to you and them both.

There are defining moments in the training room. They arrive through hard work on your part, good materials, some luck, and even the presence of karma or kismet—that moment when you know they are yours and you can take them where you want them to go. Good luck and good training. Break a leg out there.

THE FOLLOWING items are included in this Appendix:

- Room Set-Up Specifications
- Small-Group, Seminar-Style Room Preferences
- Pre-Training Worksheet
- Trainer's Travel Checklist

ROOM SET-UP SPECIFICATIONS

Tough training topics don't compete too well with bad room set-ups. The more uncomfortable the participants are, the more they will take it out on you, either during the session or via the feedback sheets.

As with many issues surrounding the training experience, the phrase, "It depends" fits here too. Your room design will depend on the type of program you're teaching, the length, and the type of work the participants will be doing. Sometimes you will have some control over the room design, and sometimes you won't. Sometimes the tables are mounted, the chairs are fixed, and you can't change anything about the fluorescent lights, which you can either turn all the way on (far too bright) or all the way off (pitch black).

If I have any say in the issue, my preference for the room design is to put the group at round tables, with about five to seven people per table. This, of course, encourages more connection between people and makes it easier and faster to do table-team exercises.

My least favorite room design is the notoriously uncomfortable row after row after row of chairs, facing forward. When these are too tightly spaced, front and back and on both sides, the participants get grouchy quickly. Plus, it's tough to sit for more than a few hours this way, taking notes on papers you hold on your lap.

My next least favorite room design is the old standby—the horseshoe. This set-up limits the amount of movement for the presenter (unless you want to climb over a table and move around in the inside) and makes it more difficult for the participants to work together effectively.

Rows of tables are a bit better, since people can take notes and sit more comfortably. If you want them to work in groups, they can simply turn to colleagues on either side and make small working groups in their rows.

SMALL-GROUP, SEMINAR-STYLE ROOM PREFERENCES

Room Design

- Table teams (five to seven people per table).
- Each table has a new easel pad, marking pens, Post-it® Notes, index cards, masking tape, name tents, water, and glasses.
- Each table will have enough space around it to allow participants to sit comfortably and move around the table and easel pad.
- There will be sufficient available wall space to put up easel pad pages.
- All participant handouts and related materials will be in place on the tables, prior to the start of the training.

Front of the Room

- Small rectangular table for the projector, laptop, and presenter's materials.
- Two new easel pads with marking pens and masking tape.
- Water and glasses.
- Portable or fixed screen.
- Access to TV/VCR, placed on a 60-inch or higher cart for best viewing.
- Power strip and extension cord.

For Programs in Hotels or Conference Centers

- No catering or restocking of sodas, coffee, and other items during the session, only during the breaks or lunch periods.
- Hotel will provide access to A/V specialist at least 45 minutes prior to the start of the presentation.
- All electrical sockets in the training room will be operational.
- Hotel will provide best available training room (not near the kitchen or employee passageways to maintenance, janitorial, or storage facilities).

PRE-TRAINING WORKSHEET

This comes from my father's office at Karl Albrecht International. It's a useful tool for training success, since it addresses a lot of little details that, left unmanaged, can make for a tough training day. Have your internal or external client fully complete this prior to your session.

"We want to make the presentation to your group as effective as possible. To do that, we need some information and assistance from you. Please let us have the following information as early as possible so we can focus the presentation on the needs of your participants and your business objectives."

Organization or department hosting the training?	
Date(s) of the training?	
Location of the training?	
Title or theme of the training?	
Has there been previous training on this topic? When?	
Proposed start time and length?	
Snacks, meals, coffee, other items provided?	
Number of people expected?	
Describe the audience. (jobs, educational levels, familiarity with the subject of the presentation)	
Are all participants fluent in English? If not, will you provide professional interpreters? What languages? Simultaneous or consecutive translations?	
Allow for questions after the presentation? How much time?	

Who will introduce the speaker? Please provide name, phone and fax numbers.	
"This will be a worthwhile session if. . . ." (please complete the sentence)	
Does another training session precede this one?	
Does another training session follow this one?	
Dress code for the speaker?	
Are there any social functions the speaker is asked to attend? (specify)	
Are there meetings in which the speaker is asked to participate? (specify)	
Who are the most senior persons involved in or attending the meeting?	
Airport for speaker arrival?	
Hotel for speaker lodging? (name, address, phone, fax)	
Will you provide the speaker's handout materials to the audience?	
Do you want to acquire any of the speaker's books for the participants? Which book? Quantity?	
Person who will receive and manage materials, if any (name, ship-to address, phone, and fax)?	
Please provide any other pertinent information that may be important in ensuring a quality session.	

TRAINER'S TRAVEL CHECKLIST

PC and Projector Bag

- ☐ Projector
- ☐ Laptop
- ☐ Power cords
- ☐ Power strip and extension cord
- ☐ Projector cable
- ☐ External mini-speakers (if required for sound)
- ☐ Spare projector bulb
- ☐ Back-up copy of program on CD-ROM or floppy disk
- ☐ Trainer's leader's guide/lecture notes
- ☐ Seminar video(s)
- ☐ Seminar notebooks or handouts
- ☐ Book(s) (giveaways, raffle, or display)
- ☐ Presenter bio sheet
- ☐ Pens, masking tape, Post-it® Notes, games, props, giveaways

Travel

- ☐ Airplane e-tickets/boarding pass(es)/itinerary
- ☐ Briefcase
- ☐ ID and/or passport (as necessary)

Personal

- ☐ Suitcase
- ☐ Clothes
- ☐ Shoes
- ☐ Belt
- ☐ Suits
- ☐ Toiletries kit
- ☐ After-hours clothes (workout, sleep, casual)

REFERENCES

Alliger, G. M., & Janak, E. A. (1989). Kirkpatrick's levels of training criteria: Thirty years later. *Personnel Psychology, 42,* 331–342.

Gardner, J. (1964). *Self-renewal: The individual and the innovative society.* New York: W. W. Norton.

James, T., & Shephard, D. (2001). *Presenting magically.* Williston, VT: Crown House Publishing.

Janove, J. W. (2003, January). Speak softly and carry a big stick. *HR Magazine,* pp. 73–74.

Albrecht, Karl. (1982). *Mindex: Your Thinking Style Profile.* San Diego, CA: Albrecht Publishing.

Albrecht, Karl. (2005). *Social Intelligence.* San Francisco, CA: Jossey-Bass.

Albrecht, Steve. (1997). *Fear and Violence on the Job.* Durham, NC: Carolina Academic Press.

Barbazette, Jean. (2001). *Successful New Employee Orientation* (2nd ed.). San Francisco, CA: Pfeiffer.

Baron, S. Anthony. (1992). *Violence in the Workplace.* Santa Barbara, CA: Pathfinder Press.

Bittel, Lester R., & Newstrom, John W. (1992). *What Every Supervisor Should Know* (6th ed.). New York: McGraw-Hill.

Carter, Carol, et al. (1999). *Keys to Success.* Boston, MA: Pearson Custom Publishing.

De Bono, Edward. (1985). *Six Thinking Hats.* Boston, MA: Little, Brown.

Drummond, Mary-Ellen. (1993). *Fearless and Flawless Public Speaking: With Power, Polish, and Pizazz.* San Francisco, CA: Pfeiffer.

Engel, Herbert M. (1994). *Handbook of Creative Training Exercises* (2nd ed.). Amherst, MA: HRD Press.

Engleberg, Isa N. (1994). *The Principles of Public Presentation.* New York: HarperCollins.

Greive, Donald. (2001). *A Handbook for Adjunct/Part-Time Faculty and Teachers of Adults* (4th ed.). Ann Arbor, MI: Info-Tec.

Greive, Donald. (Ed.). (2003). *Handbook II: Advanced Teaching Strategies for Adjunct/Part-Time Faculty.* Ann Arbor, MI: Info-Tec.

Gross, Ronald. (1999). *Peak Learning.* New York: Tarcher/Putnam.

Grote, Dick. (1995). *Discipline Without Punishment.* New York: AMACOM.

Hoff, Ron. (1992). *I Can See You Naked.* Kansas City, MO: Andrews and McMeel.

James, Tad, & Shephard, David. (2001). *Presenting Magically.* Williston, VT: Crown House Publishing.

Klepper, Michael. (1994). *I'd Rather Die Than Give a Speech.* Burr Ridge, IL: Irwin Professional Publishing.

Lucas, Robert William. (2000). *The Big Book of Flip Charts.* New York: McGraw-Hill.

Millbower, Lenn. (2003). *Showbiz Training.* New York: AMACOM.

Munson, Lawrence S. (1992). *How to Conduct Training Seminars* (2nd ed.). New York: McGraw-Hill.

Nilson, Carolyn. (1998). *More Team Games for Trainers.* New York: McGraw-Hill.

Nilson, Carolyn. (2004). *The AMA Trainers' Activity Book.* New York: AMACOM.

Powers, John H. (1994). *Public Speaking.* New York: HarperCollins.

Shore, Sandi. (2004). *Secrets to Standup Success.* Cincinnati, OH: Emmis Publishing.

Swenson, Craig. (Ed.) (2000). *Tools for Teams.* Boston, MA: Pearson Custom Publishing.

Vidakovich, Jim. (2000). *Trainers in Motion.* New York: AMACOM.

Vorhaus, John. (1994). *The Comic Toolbox.* Los Angeles, CA: Silman-James Press.

Weiss, Donald H. (2000). *Fair, Square & Legal* (3rd ed.). New York: AMACOM.

Dr. Steve Albrecht, PHR, CPP, is an author, seminar leader, and HR consultant from San Diego, California. He is the Managing Director for Albrecht Training & Development, a training and consulting firm specializing in high-risk HR issues, employee coaching, management and supervisory training, HR support, and the assessment of serious employee behavioral problems. He has been a trainer since 1987.

He holds a doctorate in Business Administration, an M.A. in Security Management, and a B.A. in English. He is board certified as a "Professional in Human Resources" (PHR) by the Society for Human Resource Management and as a "Certified Protection Professional" (CPP) by the American Society for Industrial Security.

His thirteen other books include *Service! Service! Service!*; *Added Value Negotiating* (with Karl Albrecht); *Ticking Bombs: Defusing Violence in the Workplace* (written in 1994 as one of the first business books on this subject); *Fear & Violence on the Job;* and four titles for law enforcement.

Steve has been a Course Leader for the American Management Association since 1997 and teaches the popular "Power Thinking for Powerful

Results" course, along with negotiation and basic supervision programs. He also serves as an adjunct professor for Criminal Justice at Chapman University.

Please contact Steve at drsteve@drstevealbrecht.com or visit his Web site at www.drstevealbrecht.com.

INDEX

A

Adult learning: and fear of failure, 42–43; generational differences in, 52–53; and individual comfort zones, 57–60; levels of reception in, 13–16; metaphorical cognitive styles of, 55–57; and neurolinguistic theory, 53–55; and trainer-participant alignment, 60; visualization techniques for, 47–49

Albrecht, K., 55–57, 245

Alcohol use: addiction and, 158; observable signs and symptoms of, 166. *See also* Substance abuse

Alliger, G. M., 13

Attendance-related behaviors, appropriate responses to, 175

Attorneys, training suggestions for, 62–63

Auditory learners, training for, 53

B

Behavioral issues, appropriate supervisory responses to, 175–176

Bio/intro sheet, 22, 38–39, 61, 62

Blanchard, K., 209

Blue-collar employees: keys to successful sessions with, 66–67; in substance abuse programs, 151

C

Closing ceremonies, 28

Closing comments, 45

Coaching interventions, 183–185; critical success factors in, 191, 192; four dimensions of, 184; methodology in, 193; skills targeted in, 190; training for, 177–178, 179–180; uses and types of, 189, 190

Conflict resolution, and individual empowerment, 209–210. *See also* Group conflict resolutions programs

Human resources: and employee orientation, 78; and substance abuse issues, 148, 149, 154–155; and supervisory training programs, 176–177; wellness programs of, 224, 226

Humor: caveats for using, 249–251; examples for using, 37, 40, 61, 100; as tension-cutting device, 131–132, 150

J

James, T., 31

Janak, E.A., 13

Judges, training sessions for, 62–63

K

Kinesthetic learners, training modes for, 54

Kirkpatrick, D., 13; Adult Learning Model of, 13–14

L

Learning formats: humor in, 3; low-stress, 41–43; variety in, 3

Learning keys, 4. *See also specific training category*

Looping back technique, 60

M

Managers. *See* Substance abuse awareness programs

Materials, handling problems with, 24

McGregor, D., 204

McGuire, J., 209

Medical doctors and nurses, training sessions for, 63–65

Mencken, H. L., 73

N

"Name Game," 58–59

Non-English speakers, keys to successful sessions with, 65–66

O

Occupational Safety and Health Administration (OSHA): safe workplace guidelines of, 127; and types of workplace violence perpetrators, 139

P

Participants, engagement techniques for, 57–60. *See also* Special category participants; Tough participants; Trainer-audience rapport

Performance evaluation training: discussion steps in, 188; in supervisory training program, 177, 179; tips, 187

Performance issues, appropriate supervisory response to, 176

Pike, R., 52

Politically correct attendees, hostile encounters with, 73–74

Pre-training worksheet, 262–263

Program content and delivery, defining, 18

Program design: "Brainy College Professor Model" for, 19–20; emphasizing content versus delivery, 16–22; infotainment as, 18; motivational speaking approach to, 19; trainer's personal style in, 20, 41–42

Progressive discipline training, 177–178, 194; counseling and, 182; model for, 195; and role-play scenarios, 181; termination and, 180

R

Review pledge, 253–254

Pfeiffer Publications Guide

This guide is designed to familiarize you with the various types of Pfeiffer publications. The formats section describes the various types of products that we publish; the methodologies section describes the many different ways that content might be provided within a product. We also provide a list of the topic areas in which we publish.

FORMATS

In addition to its extensive book-publishing program, Pfeiffer offers content in an array of formats, from fieldbooks for the practitioner to complete, ready-to-use training packages that support group learning.

FIELDBOOK Designed to provide information and guidance to practitioners in the midst of action. Most fieldbooks are companions to another, sometimes earlier, work, from which its ideas are derived; the fieldbook makes practical what was theoretical in the original text. Fieldbooks can certainly be read from cover to cover. More likely, though, you'll find yourself bouncing around following a particular theme, or dipping in as the mood, and the situation, dictate.

HANDBOOK A contributed volume of work on a single topic, comprising an eclectic mix of ideas, case studies, and best practices sourced by practitioners and experts in the field.

An editor or team of editors usually is appointed to seek out contributors and to evaluate content for relevance to the topic. Think of a handbook not as a ready-to-eat meal, but as a cookbook of ingredients that enables you to create the most fitting experience for the occasion.

RESOURCE Materials designed to support group learning. They come in many forms: a complete, ready-to-use exercise (such as a game); a comprehensive resource on one topic (such as conflict management) containing a variety of methods and approaches; or a collection of like-minded activities (such as icebreakers) on multiple subjects and situations.

TRAINING PACKAGE An entire, ready-to-use learning program that focuses on a particular topic or skill. All packages comprise a guide for the facilitator/trainer and a workbook for the participants. Some packages are supported with additional media—such as video—or learning aids, instruments, or other devices to help participants understand concepts or practice and develop skills.

- *Facilitator/trainer's guide* Contains an introduction to the program, advice on how to organize and facilitate the learning event, and step-by-step instructor notes. The guide also contains copies of presentation materials—handouts, presentations, and overhead designs, for example—used in the program.

- *Participant's workbook* Contains exercises and reading materials that support the learning goal and serves as a valuable reference and support guide for participants in the weeks and months that follow the learning event. Typically, each participant will require his or her own workbook.

ELECTRONIC CD-ROMs and Web-based products transform static Pfeiffer content into dynamic, interactive experiences. Designed to take advantage of the searchability, automation, and ease-of-use that technology provides, our e-products bring convenience and immediate accessibility to your workspace.

METHODOLOGIES

CASE STUDY A presentation, in narrative form, of an actual event that has occurred inside an organization. Case studies are not prescriptive, nor are they used to prove a point; they are designed to develop critical analysis and decision-making skills. A case study has a specific time frame, specifies a sequence of events, is narrative in structure, and contains a plot structure—an issue (what should be/have been done?). Use case studies when the goal is to enable participants to apply previously learned theories to the circumstances in the case, decide what is pertinent, identify the real issues, decide what should have been done, and develop a plan of action.

ENERGIZER A short activity that develops readiness for the next session or learning event. Energizers are most commonly used after a break or lunch to stimulate or refocus the group. Many involve some form of physical activity, so they are a useful way to counter post-lunch lethargy. Other uses include transitioning from one topic to another, where "mental" distancing is important.

EXPERIENTIAL LEARNING ACTIVITY (ELA) A facilitator-led intervention that moves participants through the learning cycle from experience to application (also known as a Structured Experience). ELAs are carefully thought-out designs in which there is a definite learning purpose and intended outcome. Each step—everything that participants do during the activity—facilitates the accomplishment of the stated goal. Each ELA includes complete instructions for facilitating the intervention and a clear statement of goals, suggested group size and timing, materials required, an explanation of the process, and, where appropriate, possible variations to the activity. (For more detail on Experiential Learning Activities, see the Introduction to the *Reference Guide to Handbooks and Annuals*, 1999 edition, Pfeiffer, San Francisco.)

GAME A group activity that has the purpose of fostering team spirit and togetherness in addition to the achievement of a pre-stated goal. Usually contrived—undertaking a desert expedition, for example—this type of learning method offers an engaging means for participants to demonstrate and practice business and interpersonal skills. Games are effective for team building and personal development mainly because the goal is subordinate to the process—the means through which participants reach decisions, collaborate, communicate, and generate trust and understanding. Games often engage teams in "friendly" competition.

ICEBREAKER A (usually) short activity designed to help participants overcome initial anxiety in a training session and/or to acquaint the participants with one another. An icebreaker can be a fun activity or can be tied to specific topics or training goals. While a useful tool in itself, the icebreaker comes into its own in situations where tension or resistance exists within a group.

INSTRUMENT A device used to assess, appraise, evaluate, describe, classify, and summarize various aspects of human behavior. The term used to describe an instrument depends primarily on its format and purpose. These terms include survey, questionnaire, inventory, diagnostic, survey, and poll. Some uses of instruments include providing instrumental feedback to group members, studying here-and-now processes or functioning within a group, manipulating group composition, and evaluating outcomes of training and other interventions.

Instruments are popular in the training and HR field because, in general, more growth can occur if an individual is provided with a method for focusing specifically on his or her own behavior. Instruments also are used to obtain information that will serve as a basis for change and to assist in workforce planning efforts.

Paper-and-pencil tests still dominate the instrument landscape with a typical package comprising a facilitator's guide, which offers advice on administering the instrument and interpreting the collected data, and an initial set of instruments. Additional instruments are available separately. Pfeiffer, though, is investing heavily in e-instruments. Electronic instrumentation provides effortless distribution and, for larger groups particularly, offers advantages over paper-and-pencil tests in the time it takes to analyze data and provide feedback.

LECTURETTE A short talk that provides an explanation of a principle, model, or process that is pertinent to the participants' current learning needs. A lecturette is intended to establish a common language bond between the trainer and the participants by providing a mutual frame of reference. Use a lecturette as an introduction to a group activity or event, as an interjection during an event, or as a handout.

MODEL A graphic depiction of a system or process and the relationship among its elements. Models provide a frame of reference and something more tangible, and more easily remembered, than a verbal explanation. They also give participants something to "go on," enabling them to track their own progress as they experience the dynamics, processes, and relationships being depicted in the model.

ROLE PLAY A technique in which people assume a role in a situation/scenario: a customer service rep in an angry-customer exchange, for example. The way in which the role is approached is then discussed and feedback is offered. The role play is often repeated using a different approach and/or incorporating changes made based on feedback received. In other words, role playing is a spontaneous interaction involving realistic behavior under artificial (and safe) conditions.

SIMULATION A methodology for understanding the interrelationships among components of a system or process. Simulations differ from games in that they test or use a model that depicts or mirrors some aspect of reality in form, if not necessarily in content. Learning occurs by studying the effects of change on one or more factors of the model. Simulations are commonly used to test hypotheses about what happens in a system—often referred to as "what if?" analysis—or to examine best-case/worst-case scenarios.

THEORY A presentation of an idea from a conjectural perspective. Theories are useful because they encourage us to examine behavior and phenomena through a different lens.

TOPICS

The twin goals of providing effective and practical solutions for workforce training and organization development and meeting the educational needs of training and human resource professionals shape Pfeiffer's publishing program. Core topics include the following:

Leadership & Management

Communication & Presentation

Coaching & Mentoring

Training & Development

e-Learning

Teams & Collaboration

OD & Strategic Planning

Human Resources

Consulting

What will you find on pfeiffer.com?

- The best in workplace performance solutions for training and HR professionals
- Downloadable training tools, exercises, and content
- Web-exclusive offers
- Training tips, articles, and news
- Seamless online ordering
- Author guidelines, information on becoming a Pfeiffer Affiliate, and much more

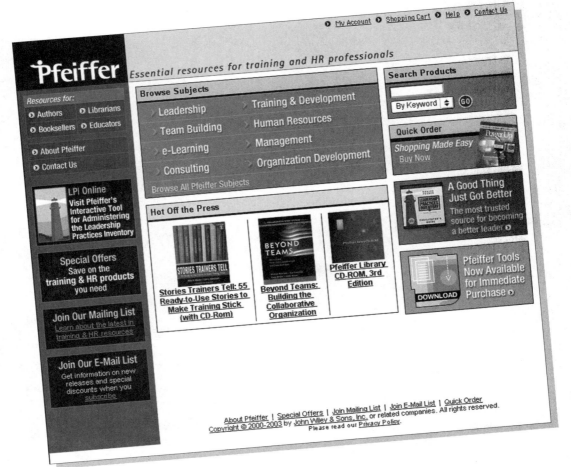

Discover more at www.pfeiffer.com